SILVIANO SANTIAGO
IN CONVERSATION

edited by
Macdonald Daly
and
Else R P Vieira

London
Spanish, Portuguese and Latin American Studies in the Humanities

ISBN 9781912399123

Silviano Santiago in Conversation
Edited by Macdonald Daly
and Else R. P. Vieira

First published in Great Britain by
Zoilus Press, 1999.

Reprinted by SPLASH Editions,
2020. SPLASH Editions is an
imprint of Jetstone Publishers Ltd.

Cover photograph by
Milton Montenegro.

Contents

FOREWORD   5
Macdonald Daly

'THE WHITE WALL': PRE-FACING SILVIANO SANTIAGO   7
Else R P Vieira

SILVIANO SANTIAGO IN CONVERSATION   15
with Else Vieira, Bernard McGuirk, Wander Miranda
and Richard King

THE PRISON-HOUSE OF MEMOIRS: SILVIANO SANTIAGO'S   26
EM liberdade
K David Jackson

SILVIANO SANTIAGO: DOUBLE STILETTO   45
Wander Melo Miranda

SILVIANO SANTIAGO: A BIBLIOGRAPHICAL NOTE   63

NOTES ON THE CONTRIBUTORS   64

FOREWORD
Macdonald Daly

This book will have served its purpose if, in introducing the work of Silviano Santiago to an English-speaking audience, it extends interest in, stimulates greater familiarity with, or encourages wider translation of his multifaceted and transgeneric corpus of texts. It aims to represent three different aspects of Santiago's work.

Else R. P. Vieira's introductory essay, as well as providing a general background, emphasizes Santiago's seminal concepts of in-betweenness and hybridity, and relates them to his specific contribution as a postmodern translator and theorist of translation.

K. David Jackson's essay, which focuses on Santiago's fiction and poetics of simulation, has been published in Randal Johnson (ed.), *Tropical Paths: Essays on Modern Brazilian Literature* (New York: Garland, 1993), pp. 199-219 and, in translation, as 'O Cárcere da Memória: *Em liberdade*, de Silviano Santiago', in Wander Melo Miranda and Eneida Maria de Souza (eds.), *Navegar é preciso, viver: escritos para Silviano Santiago* (Belo Horizonte: Editora UFMG, Salvador: EDUFBA; Niterói: EDUFF, 1997), pp. 89-110.

Wander Melo Miranda's contribution is a version of an essay first published in pamphlet form as *Silviano Santiago: Duplo Estilete* (Belo Horizonte: Editora UFMG, 1993), and offers a survey of Santiago's critical work.

The conversation with Silviano Santiago took place at the Transcultural(C)ities Colloquium, University of Nottingham, on 15 September 1998. The colloquium was sponsored by the project *The Interface of Critical and Cultural Studies* of the Federal University of Minas Gerais and the Postgraduate School of Critical Theory and Cultural Studies, University of Nottingham, funded by CAPES and the British Council, and co-ordinated by Bernard McGuirk and Else Vieira.

We acknowledge our thanks to Wander Melo Miranda and Eneida Maria de Souza for their permission to reproduce in this volume items from the bibliography of Silviano Santiago in *Navegar é preciso, viver: escritos para Silviano Santiago*. Finally, the editors are very grateful for the inestimable help of Trudie McGuirk and Richard Spurr with aspects of translation and transcription respectively.

Macdonald Daly
Nottingham
September 1999

'THE WHITE WALL': PRE-FACING
SILVIANO SANTIAGO
Else R P Vieira

Lucid, eclectic, up-to-date, rebellious, tenacious, scholarly — these are recurrent adjectives in writings on Silviano Santiago. As a critic, he is best known for three collections of essays: *Uma literatura nos trópicos: Ensaios sobre dependência cultural* [*A Literature in the Tropics: Essays on Cultural Dependence*] (1978), *Vale quanto pesa: ensaios sobre questões político-culturais* [*It is Worth its Weight: Essays on Political and Cultural Questions*] (1982), and *Nas malhas da letra: ensaios* [*In the Weavings [Fabric/Mesh] of the Letter: Essays*] (1989). In *Uma literatura nos trópicos*, he advanced two seminal concepts that have since illuminated many studies and reflections on Brazilian and Latin American literatures and cultures: in-betweenness and hybridity. Not a dichotomy but a duality, in-betweenness has been seen as his groundbreaking concept, one that was conceived initially as a way of describing the role of the Latin American artist away from parameters of cultural dependence: a relation grounded not on binary oppositions but operating at the threshold of fusion and distinction, assimilation and expropriation. Silviano Santiago is further known for having opened Brazilian fiction to postmodernity and for his mastery of pastiche and the dimensions of fake biographies. His most widely read fictional productions, in Brazil and abroad, are *Em liberdade* [*In Liberty*] (1981), *Stella Manhattan* (1994), and *Viagem ao México* [*A Trip to Mexico*] (1995). As a translator, he started with Samuel Beckett's *Fin de partie* (1959), having also translated Jacques Prévert's poems (1985) and Robbe-Grillet's *Pour quoi j'aime Barthes?* (1995) into Portuguese. His main theoretical contribution to translation theory has been the development of the notion of double plagiarism, a project that conceives of translation as a matter of bilateral absorption and which, in another context, bears affinities with Deleuze's 'double capture', in that both describe a relation whereby both terms take on qualities of the other, while maintaining an independent identity. As will be seen, double plagiarism implies, more specifically, the taking on of properties from both the original literature and the receiving literature. The translated text thus emerges as a *locus* of encounter of two traditions, authorships and authorities.

Roots, Routes, Reflections: an echo of the 1998 Conference, held 'offshore' in Portugal, upon the quincentenary of Vasco da Gama's voyage, and of which Santiago was the distinguished opening plenarist, further provides me with three metaphors to introduce to an English-speaking audience his multifaceted career as a critic, novelist, professor

In Conversation

and translation theorist.[1] In each of these trajectories, he is acclaimed for having unveiled spaces of liminality, by blurring the distinction between history and fiction in his novels; by exploring multiple *loci* of enunciation; or by stressing the encounter of literatures and redistributing concepts of authorship in his reflections on translation.

Some of Santiago's critics perceive Belo Horizonte, the capital of the centrally located state of Minas Gerais, to be his roots, even though he was born in the nearby town of Formiga, in 1936.[2] It was in Belo Horizonte that Santiago made the first *entrées* into a literary career. He took a bachelor's degree in Romance languages from the University of Minas Gerais, where he helped to set up and publish the journal *Complemento*, which was an outlet for his early short stories; it was also for the stages of Belo Horizonte that he translated Beckett. If there are those who claim his roots, Santiago himself will ever trace routes, which finds an echo in Hoisel's view of his life as one that constructs itself through trajectories. Man is constantly in movement, he says, and the wealth of his multiple *loci* of enunciation can be seen then to derive more from such routes:

> [Santiago] does not opt for a fixed point, one centre from which to articulate his voice. If knowledge is mobile, Santiago stresses its mobility in these processes of successive migrations. (Hoisel in Miranda and de Souza, 1997: 44).

In 1960 Santiago moved to Rio de Janeiro to pursue a course of studies on French Literature, and there he stayed until given an award by the French government to pursue a Ph.D degree at the Sorbonne, where he wrote a thesis on André Gide. From France he moved to North America, where he embarked upon a University career, beginning in New Mexico, then at Rutgers, at the University of Toronto, and at the State University of New York at Buffalo. He also taught in Paris at the Sorbonne Nouvelle.

1974 was a year of reflections and redirections. He decided to return to his home country, Brazil. But the previous routes accompanied him in this renewed encounter with his first *locus* of enunciation. Upon his

---

[1] *Roots, Routes, Reflections: 1498-1998*, conference of The Association of Hispanists of Great Britain and Ireland, Universidade do Minho, Braga, Portugal, September 1998.

[2] For the biographical information throughout this preface, I acknowledge my debt to the 'Chronology of Silviano Santiago' (Miranda and de Souza, 1997: 322-36).

return, he lectured at the Catholic University of Rio de Janeiro, then at the Federal University of Rio de Janeiro and at the Federal Fluminense University in Niterói. It was in the period of work at the Catholic University that he started disseminating Jacques Derrida in Brazil, a role akin to that of Gayatri Spivak in the United States, as the translator of Derrida into English; he co-ordinated the compilation of a glossary on Derrida, published in 1976.

Yet Brazil was more than a place of residence and work. In his renewed reflections, Brazil becomes the stuff of his writing, a metaphor: the blank wall on which to write. Santiago's metaphors, like his personality, his criticism, his fiction, his scholarship, will often startle his reader. Always at the tip of his tongue, these metaphors are just waiting for the ear of the other to interpret them at will. One might expect the white wall Santiago sees in front of him upon his return to Brazil, after 12 years abroad, to mean nothingness, which remains a possibility. Yet, Santiago himself was to provide another interpretation. The white wall is one on which he could write about Brazil and Latin America. This perception grew in definition after he had been teaching French literature in Buffalo for three years. Having not spoken Portuguese all this time, he went through the strange experience of being, in a way, an outsider, losing his own language. As becomes apparent in the discussion reproduced as the final item in this collection, Santiago, of Italian descent, and having lived abroad for so many years, has the experience of foreignness before becoming aware of his Brazilianness. In this context, the white wall takes on another meaning; it is an inscription that pre-faced him, that pre-figured his own way of thinking Brazilian and Latin American traditions, but of which he had not been aware. Upon his return, he begins to decipher, to write about what was already there on that white wall. This meant not quite creating a place, but a situation that he calls '*o entre-lugar*', in-betweenness. What was a personal experience develops into a seminal critical concept for Latin America. In-betweenness, that liminal *locus* of the Latin American artist, is thus cast by Santiago:

> Between sacrifice and play, between prison and transgression, between submission and aggression to the code, between obedience and rebellion, between assimilation and expression -- there, in this seemingly empty place, its temple and its site of clandestinity, the anthropophagous ritual of Latin America is performed. (Santiago, 1978: 28)

In Conversation

As a critic and essay writer on cultural dependence, again moving beyond binaries and further stressing the dimensions of power, he proposes a related concept, that of hybridity, which describes the condition of liminality of postcolonial cultures. The context is the moment at which he brings to visibility the contribution of Latin America in breaking with the Western view of purity and unity as a claim to superiority. He thus stresses deviation from the norm and contamination as the role of Latin America:

> Colonial Renaissance engenders [...] a new society, that of the *mestizos*, whose main characteristic is that the notion of unity is overturned, it is contaminated in favour of a subtle and complex mixture between the European and the autochthonous element. In this new and untiring movement of opposition, of racial staining, of sabotage of the cultural and social values imposed by the Conquerors, a greater transformation takes place on the surface but which definitely affects the correction of the main systems that contributed to the propagation of Western culture between us: the linguistic and the religious codes. These codes lose their status of purity and little by little allow themselves to be enriched by new acquisitions, by minute metamorphoses, by strange corruptions, that transform the integrity of the European Holy Book and of the Dictionary and the Grammar. The hybrid element reigns. (Santiago, 1978: 17-18)

It remains to consider Santiago's use of pastiche in fiction in connection with his development, as a postmodern translator and translation theorist, of the notion of double plagiarism, devised as he theorized upon his translation of Prévert into Portuguese.

What is a translator? What is a postmodern translator? Three decades have passed since the world was confronted with the problematization of authorship, subjectivity and so on, as has been the case, for example, with Foucault's 'What is an author?'. Over a decade has passed since the world was confronted with the problematization of copyrights in translation, as has been the case with Derrida's *Des tours de Babel*. Yet the responses to these challenges in translation theory have been at least patchy. How do Santiago's prefaces as a postmodern translator and novelist shed light on the issue? How do they accommodate the view of the text as a weave of voices? How are the voices of the translator and fiction writer to be understood as a supplement to earlier voices?

For Santiago, origin and unity are no longer the reference, and his prefaces, as a matter of fact, shake the notions of one individual as the one possessor of his writing. Reminiscing Foucault's questionings, 'work' for Santiago becomes problematic if thought of as a unit. The names Silviano Santiago and Graciliano Ramos, or, as we shall see in relation to translation, Silviano Santiago and Jacques Prévert, interrelate rather than authenticate authorship, which thus emerges as a plurality of 'I's. His attribution of the memoirs of *Em liberdade* [*In Liberty*] to Graciliano Ramos, the author actually of *Memórias do cárcere* [*Prison Memoirs*], does not parallel the attribution of a discourse to him; the discourse remains Santiago's. Graciliano Ramos is, in fact, supplemented when Silviano Santiago writes the diary he might have written after serving his term in jail. Introducing himself as the editor of the manuscripts that were sent to him to be published anonymously twenty-five years after Ramos's death, Santiago thus establishes a politics of proper names that effaces the distinction between primary and secondary models, and also auto- and hetero-biography. It is not the author who becomes the source of authority. As Barthes would say, 'to give a text an Author is to impose a limit on that text' (Barthes, 1977: 147). It is form that indeed becomes the limit, the prison that further establishes a contrast with the liberty of creating which, in turn, stands as a contrast to the real experience of the earlier writer in jail. Santiago thus presents the manuscript as fake writing, after having spent months training himself in the style of this great deceased author and developing what K. David Jackson has highlighted in *Em liberdade* as the aesthetics of simulation (Jackson, in this volume).

Shedding another perspective on authorship away from individuality, further problematising ownership in writing, Santiago subtitles his novel 'A Fiction by Silviano Santiago'. It is to be noticed that rather than establishing a pact of authorial truth, he highlights the fictionality of authorship. His epigraph from Otto Maria Carpeaux, 'I shall construct my Graciliano Ramos', further highlights the role of the author as a weaver of voices, the new text emerging as a transformation of the other, transformation here understood as complementation and supplementation of the work. A continued existence is through Santiago's fiction stressed by the note of the editor (also Silviano Santiago), who begins with a description of Ramos's arrest and of the circumstances in which he was set free, how he 'wrote his diary' and gave it to a friend for burning; the friend, however, kept the originals and one month after Ramos's death in Rio de Janeiro, having the chance to meet Santiago, gave them to him. Santiago kept it in secret before publishing them. All the concrete details of Ramos and his diary that apparently build a pact of truth are demythified as the 'editor' finally

In Conversation

closes the preface stating that 'all the responsibility of this publication lies with this signatory', Silviano Santiago. Again calling attention to the elusiveness of authorship, Santiago re-establishes a pact of veracity, writing a note on this edition, remarking on minor corrections to Ramos's typing, on the typically circumstantial style of the diary. And there is an explanation for Ramos's wish to have the originals burned that stresses the multiplicity of 'I's in writing: *In Liberty* and *Prison Memoirs* do not match, 'they could not coexist simultaneously in his mind'. Authorship disperses, multiplicity is emphasized through fiction, explanations move away from origin towards continuation.

What of translation? The technique of pastiche that undermines the concept of model re-emerges in his theorization of translation. The dichotomies true and false, original and copy, are further questioned in Santiago's view of translation. The text to be translated is Prévert's but the form and diction used are those of Brazilian poets. Santiago analyses the prominent aspects of Prévert's poetry and concludes that his diction, colloquial style, and striking humour bear resemblances to the Brazilian poets of the 1930s, who, having abandoned the aggressive and avant-garde tone of poetry in the 1920s, still keep a colloquial syntax and lexicon. Hence his reconceptualising of the notion of model in translation:

> It was after 'models' such as Manuel Bandeira, Carlos Drummond de Andrade and Murilo Mendes that we attempted to transpose Prévert's verses into Portuguese (...). It was the translator's task not to impose on the text to be translated a poetic diction that would explain the poem, but to search in the repertoire of possible dictions in the national literature an equivalent that would be just. (Santiago in Prévert, 1988: 11)

Using Santiago's own words as a critic and essayist on hybridity, one could say that Brazilian literature comes to contaminate Prévert; or even within the Benjaminian metaphor elaborated by Derrida, one could say that Santiago wraps Prévert with the robe of Manuel Bandeira and Carlos Drummond de Andrade. Santiago does not translate only into a language, he translates into a literature. He thus advances the notion of double plagiarism:

> In this sense, this translator is an exegete with clipped wings, certainly a double plagiarist. He plagiarizes the text to be translated and plagiarizes the national poets that he selected as models of translation. (Santiago in Prévert, 1988: 11)

Faking identities, exposing multiplicity rather than unity, one voice complementing and supplementing the other is what becomes apparent in Santiago's translation of Prévert and in his fiction *In Liberty*. Echoing Foucault, it could be said that, rather than original authors, Prévert's and Ramos's discourses are founders of discursivity, in that they produce the possibility and the rule of formation of other texts, establishing an infinite possibility of discourses (Foucault, 1992: 58). They open the room for something different from them and that, nonetheless, belongs with what they have founded. Rather than a 'copy' of the other, a relationship of becoming is established. The last version thus holds a plurality of 'I's; attribution then does not point to one individual but gives way to various 'I's simultaneously; authorship is disseminated.

It is finally worth noting the ambiguity of the metaphor for freedom in his translation project, in that it already contains a form of imprisonment: the wings allow for movement but, because clipped, restricted movement. This metaphor interweaves with a subtle allusion to Oswald de Andrade, associated with the movement of Cannibalism in Brazil, which reverberates in Santiago's definition of translation as 'transgression with a plea for forgiveness, ownership without copyrights'. As K. David Jackson says in relation to *Em liberdade,* freedom only leads to its opposite — other forms of prison — be they language or literary genre.

Like a white wall pre-figuring writing....

In Conversation

REFERENCES

Barthes, Roland. 'The Death of the Author', in *Image-Music-Text*, tr. Stephen Heath (London: Fontana Press, 1977).

Foucault, Michel. *O que é um autor?*, tr. António Fernando Cascais and Eduardo Cordeiro (Vega, Passagens, 1992).

Graham, Joseph. *Difference in Translation* (Ithaca: Cornell University Press, 1985).

Miranda, Wander Melo and Souza, Eneida Maria de (eds.). *Navegar é preciso, viver: escritos para Silviano Santiago* (Belo Horizonte: Editora UFMG; Salvador: EDUFBA; Niterói: EDUFF, 1997).

Miranda, Wander Melo. *Corpos escritos: Graciliano Ramos e Silviano Santiago* (São Paulo: Editora da Universidade de São Paulo; Belo Horizonte: Editora UFMG, 1992).

Prévert, Jacques. *Poemas*, tr. Silviano Santiago (Rio de Janeiro: Nova Fronteira, 1988).

Santiago, Silviano. *Uma literatura nos trópicos: ensaios de dependência cultural* (São Paulo: Editora Perspectiva, 1978).

Santiago, Silviano. *Vale quanto pesa: ensaios sobre questões político-culturais* (Rio de Janeiro: Paz e Terra, 1982).

Santiago, Silviano. *Nas malhas da letra: ensaios* (São Paulo: Companhia das Letras, 1989).

Santiago, Silviano. *Em liberdade: uma ficção de Silviano Santiago* (Rio de Janeiro: Rocco, 1994).

Vieira, Else Ribeiro Pires. 'A Postmodern Translational Aesthetics in Brazil', in *Translation Studies: An Interdiscipline*, ed. M. Snell-Hornby, F. Pöchhacker and K. Kaindl (Amsterdam and Philadelphia: John Benjamins, 1984), 65-72.

ELSE VIEIRA: Silviano Santiago needs no introduction, so renowned is he as a critic and as a writer. He has had a long career as a professor in Brazil and in the United States, and his publications are as prolific as, of course, they are of high quality. When I asked him, 'Silviano, how would you like me to introduce you?', he said, 'Just say three words: that I'm a critic, a writer, and a professor.' So I'll stick to this request for simplicity and his eminence as critic, writer and professor will be evident enough, I think, as he talks.

We shall, in principle, restrict ourselves to four basic questions, for which we have the privilege of having with us Richard King, Professor of American Intellectual History here in the Department of American and Canadian Studies, who currently has a research project on 'Ideas of Racism between 1945 and 1970'. We have Wander Miranda, Professor of Critical Theory at the Federal University of Minas Gerais. Wander is the director of the UFMG University Press, and he is also the convenor of a project, funded by the Rockefeller Foundation, on Late Modernities in Brazil. We also have Bernard McGuirk — I suppose he requires no introduction either, but he is Professor of Romance Literatures and Literary Theory here at Nottingham University. He has published wild... err, widely, and... (we are tired... or perhaps Freud might explain it!) his most recent book, on poststucturalism and Latin-American literature, came out last year from Routledge. So I suppose we can proceed. Would you like to begin, Bernard?

BERNARD McGUIRK: One of the reasons I prefer to dispense with introductions of this kind is because I'm all too aware that, though Freud is important, so Lacan also knew about lapses in Freud. And even wildness has to be structured. The best way of controlling any hint of wildness, and any illusion that there is a kind of irresponsibility in critical theory, is to go back to literature. And I'm going to do precisely that. There can be no better way, when inviting such a distinguished colleague and friend as Silviano Santiago, than to begin with his own words. I'm going to speak to you for a moment in his language, in a different voicing, of course, and then, in English, say what it means, and ask him my question. I've chosen from his many books *Viagem ao Mexico*, as follows. Silviano, deep into the book, says: 'Nada melhor do que iniciar o seu contato com os mexicanos pela exposição oral da sua maneira de pensar a cultura, a cultura francesa atual e o México'. He says: 'Nothing better than to initiate contact with the Mexicans through the oral expression of their way of thinking culture, contemporary French culture

In Conversation

and Mexico's'. Let's transfer, in that double-stiletto relationship, which Wander Miranda has underlined in your work, by asking you to contemplate some of the dialogue which you, Silviano, have established, not with a living writer, but with Antonin Artaud. And I would suggest that we could think about this meditation of yours as a journey, not only to Mexico, of course, but also as a metaphorical voyage. At one point early in the book, you say, or someone says (after all, it's *écriture*), 'Preciso sair de dentro de mim: a vida me sufoca, carboniza a minha vontade, esteriliza a minha arte'. So the words say, 'I need to get out of myself, life suffocates me, carbonizes my will, sterilizes my art'. In that vein which you have had throughout your distinguished career, as a writer recognized in France, in the United States, and way beyond your own frontiers, there has always been a tension. You come back to Brazil. Many writers of Latin America, many distinguished critics and authors (Silviano is poet, novelist, essayist, critic) have opted to leave, and not to come back, but you have always gone back, and now, I believe, you have decided to stay there, and that you are finding, or re-finding, roots, ever more deeply in your own early life, in your own experience, which have been transcribed in so many of your books. So I'd like you to talk to us a little about *non*-exile.

SILVIANO SANTIAGO: I think that I have to start with some biographical information. I am of Italian descent, and in that respect, I was not sure of being a Brazilian for a while, and I learned to be a Brazilian, in the same way that you learn how to write, that you learn how to publish a book — it's not easy to publish a book — and I learned that. So, it's very strange, because I had an experience of foreign countries before I had an experience of Brazil. I left Brazil very early, I left Brazil in 1960, I went to France to do a doctorate, and from France I decided to go to the United States, and I worked there for many years, from '61 through '74, when I returned to Brazil. So what I believe is interesting is the fact that I didn't feel, at the beginning, that I was exiled in France, or I was exiled in Europe. I felt very comfortable not to be in Brazil. That was a very strange sensation. But the more I lived outside Brazil, the more I discovered that there was a kind of white wall in front of me, and I didn't know how to decipher that white wall, and I began to decipher it when I returned to Brazil in, if I'm not wrong, 1970 or 1971. I discovered that there were certain things that were written on that white wall, and that I was able finally to read what they were saying. And since then, what I have been doing is trying to write what I read on that wall, and I'm using 'white' wall and not 'black' wall, because it's not a teaching experience, it's not the kind of experience that you have on a

16

black-board. It's an experience that you have with yourself, and when you try to understand that what's important is basically an inscription of your own way of thinking a tradition. And that tradition to me (that's the white wall) was Brazilian literature, or Latin-American literature in a broader sense. So, from that moment on, I realized that I did not have a place, I was not a Brazilian, I was not, you know, a Brazilian of Italian descent, I was not an Italian who had gone to Europe to get a degree, and then to the United States to make some money teaching. I discovered that I was creating a place that was not a place... it was an in-between situation, and this was very important to me. There was an article that I wrote in 1971 that is called 'The In-betweenness of Latin American Literature', because the point was not to write a kind of *ufanista* or, let's say, a nationalistic Brazilian literature, and I realized also that to be cosmopolitan is too simple. (I know that I'm also teasing, but let me open this parenthesis by saying — I should *start* by saying — that Fernando Pessoa said that all poets are *fingidores* — feigners — and, I've had a lot of wine, *in vino veritas*, so most of the things I'm saying might be a glass of lies, or... a glass of truth. Anyway, I close the parenthesis.) And this in-between situation was very important to me. It was a fact that... I would say to you, Bernard, as we are very sincere... the question of exile does not exist for me. Because man is constantly on the move... man is constantly in movement, and what's important to me is that constant moving, that incapacity to create a place in which I'm going to feel comfortable. Lately, I have been reading a lot of Bruce Chatwin, and I'm finding certain affinities with Chatwin. You know, I haven't read him before — perhaps my fault. But anyway, this is a very important thing... I'll stop here, then.

WANDER MIRANDA: I have a small question for Silviano...

SILVIANO SANTIAGO: Oh, everyone has small questions. Most of them have small answers!

WANDER MIRANDA: No, it's very, very small — what's fiction for you?

SILVIANO: What's fiction? Oh my gosh.

WANDER MIRANDA: The second part is what's the place of Brazil in your fiction?

SILVIANO SANTIAGO: Fiction to me is something extremely

17

In Conversation

elaborate, I have to say, it's not simple. One of my — here I'll have to pay some compliments to myself — one of the books I like, one of my novels, is called *Em liberdade*, and it's a pastiche (the word exists in English, doesn't it?), it's a pastiche of a Brazilian novelist called Graciliano Ramos. Graciliano Ramos, during the '30s, was in jail and he published four volumes that he called *Memoirs from Prison* and I decided, in 1975-1976, to write a fake diary of Graciliano Ramos that I called *In Freedom* — I mean, what he would have written when he left prison. Because the basic point of fiction to me is the question of freedom, that's the basic question to me, and freedom in Brazil is almost a utopian situation, so I decided to write fiction as if freedom were within imprisoned forms (what I call 'imprisoned forms', because it's a pastiche). So I was using his style, for six months. I learned how to write… you know, the way he writes… and after six months, then I started writing the novel. And that I shall call a kind of 'imprisoned form' — how can you find a certain freedom within an imprisoned form? So form was not something that existed in a kind of 'free' way, which was simply there, that you could touch with your hands. It was not something that you could copy, not something that you could emulate. Form exists in a very strong and precise shape, and I had to find my way, working through that very strong and precise shape. In other words, I had to invent freedom; freedom is something that you invent. And I move now, I think, to your second question. I think that, inventing freedom, I'm becoming a Brazilian writer, I'm becoming a Brazilian intellectual, I'm talking about Brazil, I'm talking about citizenship, I'm talking of the possibility of surviving in a country, or in a region, that is constantly affected by dictatorship. So that's your 'simple question'.

WANDER MIRANDA: That's very good, thank you.

ELSE VIEIRA: My question will be simple too…

SILVIANO SANTIAGO: Every one is simple! My goodness.

ELSE VIEIRA: First it has to do with what we might call the paradoxes of post-modernity. And the reason I bring this up is that I thought it was in 1978 that Silviano Santiago had introduced such important concepts as in-betweenness and hybridity. And, later, other of his concepts were to emerge, and here, of course, I am talking about the critic and the theorist. Some of these concepts have become part of the critical agenda in the world today, such as hybridity, in-betweenness, as explored by

Homi Bhabha. They're not quite the same but are somehow related. At this point, it looks as though Silviano Santiago has rejected these concepts, or he will not make use of them any more; they seem to belong to his past. So if you could please talk a little about this paradox, Silviano, that, just when a concept you yourself had anticipated so long ago has become such an integral part of the critical agenda, you seem to have given it up.

SILVIANO SANTIAGO: The true answer is very simple — it's just that I became old. So, I'm old. If I'm old, I think in a different way; life is different for me right now, my understanding of literature is different right now. I think that the book Bernard talked about, about a trip to Mexico, perhaps represents more what I think about that kind of concept — it's a very strange book, like the other one I mentioned to you — I write strange novels — and everyone knows that Artaud travelled to Mexico in 1936, and he visited the northern region of Mexico where the Tarahumara Indians live, and he was in Mexico City for seven, nine, months, and I thought that that was an excellent moment to talk about the relationship between a Brazilian intellectual and a French intellectual, and not in Brazil but in Mexico. So I thought that here was a good way of discussing in-betweenness, but more subtly. Because, on the one hand, what was important for me was that I became more and more politicized, I have to say, and I became more and more interested in economic questions. And what was important to me was the understanding of the thirties as the moment in which, in Brazil, the Nation State became the important tool in the creation of industry. The Nation State was a form of national economy. And Artaud was exactly the opposite. Artaud had chosen to travel to Mexico at the wrong moment, when his ideas about the Aztecs, or the myth, could not be accepted by the President of Mexico, who was interested exactly in transforming the Indians into workers, and trying to give an education to them. And that was the play I was using. And, at the same time, I could not write the book from the perspective of the thirties — the narrator is myself in the nineties. So, in the nineties, what we discovered was that new liberalism is the end of this economic trend in which the Nation State becomes less and less important, becomes minimal. So it is, you know, in that sense that I'm becoming old, I'm changing my ideas, or I'm trying to. I see the world, and the ways that ideas circulate, and the ways in which you can understand the relationship between Europe and Latin America. Europe, Latin America and Brazil are different, in that respect, you know. I like my article, but it's a 1971 article. I prefer things that I am writing today, and the book I wrote after that one, for instance.

It was for the first time a very personal book — it's about disease, and I thought it was important also to understand that there were certain themes that are personal and that perhaps I was hiding, and I should not hide, and this is called *Uma história de família*. For the first time I was trying to achieve an autobiographical writing and I thought it was important since, you know, I was doing a kind of fake writing all the time. Faking the style of Graciliano Ramos, faking the style of Artaud, faking the style of everyone, and suddenly I said, 'Why don't I fake my own style?' and I did something about it, what I would call autobiography, but actually, to tell the truth, it's the biography of my younger brother, it's not mine. It's because mine, I thought, was less interesting than his. No, it's true, he has had a very interesting life. I love him because he's — I'm not a passionate person, I'm a kind of intellectual who lives in between four walls — and he's exactly the opposite. He belonged to the Communist Party, he was in jail, you know, he suffered a lot for six months, and he had all kinds of — my mother died — I mean, this is the basic point — my mother died when she gave birth to him, and this is a book about that. And my mother did not die when she gave birth to me, and so I believe that his life is much more interesting than mine, and what I do. That's why I call it fake autobiography, because I'm not writing my autobiography, even though I give the impression that this is my autobiography, it's the biography of my brother — a person that I love a lot — and he's quite a character, and I'm not.

RICHARD KING: I'm interested in this, and it relates to Wander's question to some extent, but I'm interested in the sense in which, well, you studied in France, you lived and taught in the United States for thirteen years, went back to Brazil. In what sense were you, in a straightforward way, afraid of losing that other homeland that writers and intellectuals talk about, and that is the language, that is Portuguese, and perhaps even Brazilian Portuguese. I don't know... American writers in the United States writing in the nineteenth century made a lot of developing an English that was different from British English, you know, there was a new vernacular, Emerson, Whitman and so forth. I don't know if that's a problem for Brazilian writers, but at least in your case, was the language itself not enough to be a homeland, so that you had to go back concretely and act — well, you obviously did — but to what extent is the language also a homeland, is that perhaps the question?

SILVIANO SANTIAGO: I think that is exactly the white wall I was talking about. It was my experience at Buffalo, a very strange experience, because I was... I am Brazilian, I was teaching French literature, and I was talking basically to the people in Comparative Literature, and I'd never use Portuguese; I didn't use Portuguese for at least three or four years, and one day, a very good friend of mine — I had written an article on Machado de Assis — a very good friend of mine, who has just died, Alexandre Eulálio, said, 'You know, the quality of your Portuguese is not as good as it used to be.' I said 'my gosh' and he pointed out, in my article, certain passages, and he was right, the quality of the language was not good, and I became scared that day, *completely* scared, and I realized that it was very nice to teach at Buffalo (Buffalo, perhaps you don't know, at that time, was the centre of structuralism, René Girard, Eugenio Donato, Michel Foucault, you name it, and they were there, Jacques Derrida, and so forth). So to me, being a Brazilian, that kind of thing was a fantastic and exhilarating experience, but at the same time, I was not part of the game, I was an outsider in a certain way — and an 'outsider' losing his language, and that was the terrible point, and that's when I said at once, when I went to Brazil and I discovered that I had in front of me a kind of white wall, that I could perhaps write nice articles. At the time, I had written an article on *La Nausée*, on Sartre, because I needed to publish articles, you know, you had to publish, and I never published that article, and I made an effort to write about *La Nausée* and I said, 'it's so silly to write about *La Nausée*, it doesn't mean anything to me, this article', and I just destroyed it, and started writing a couple of short stories that eventually were called *O banquete* and things like that. But I believe that I take language not in an abstract manner, as some philosophers used to do, like 'Littérature, c'est du langage', you know, 'Literature is language'. No, I mean, language to me, is something more concrete, it is a kind of adjective, because you have constantly to elaborate what I called before a tradition. I work within a tradition, and within that tradition, I work with what I have called imprisoned forms ('formas prisioneiras') so this is a long way round, it's not like having a nice language or a neat rhetorical capacity of dealing with rhetoric, or something like that.

ELSE VIEIRA: Silviano, we had decided on one question per person, but I would just like to ask one more. There is another important point in your career, too, that is your introduction of Derrida to Brazil. How do you look back on this part of your trajectory today?

SILVIANO SANTIAGO: I shall give a complex answer. What I believe is important in my career is not the fact that I do work that's personal,

In Conversation

it's the fact that I have been able to work with so many people in Brazil. I think that if anyone asked me what is my complete works, I would say that it is what I have written with my name on it and also what most of my students have written, because I have been working closely with a good number of them. I have directed fifty dissertations — Ph.D and MA — and that's a lot. I mean, if you do that kind of work, that *is* a lot, and especially because I read them line by line and I comment line by line, and so I believe that's very important to understanding my work, and it's interesting because in a certain way I transfer to someone else who can do a better job than I do, than I might do. I think that, if I have a quality, this is my quality, the capacity to discover in someone else qualities better than mine, and to say to this person that you should do this, because if you do so, you do better work than I, obviously, and fantastic work, that's going to be a very fine contribution. And I believe that most of the dissertations I have directed have been published, are today in book form and are major contributions to Brazilian criticism, and it makes me extremely happy that I have been able to do that. You know, to discover in someone else this capacity to deal with certain questions that I'm poor at, or I'm afraid of, or I'm scared by, or I'm unprepared for, or I don't have time for, it depends — each situation is different — but I enjoy very much finding someone who's very brave and to whom I give a very difficult topic, and discover finally that he or she did a beautiful job — I enjoy that very much — it's got a kind of *voyeur* thing about it.

MACDONALD DALY: I was wondering, Silviano, what other affinities or influences there are in your work.

SILVIANO SANTIAGO: Again, I'll go back to Buffalo, because that may simplify things a bit as people in general know American literature quite well. When I was in Buffalo, I became… I don't know if I shall use the word 'friends' because he's quite a character, and a very difficult character, with a man called John Barth, very difficult, my gosh, very nice at the beginning, and then suddenly strange. And John Barth was extremely important to me, extremely important — from just a couple of conversations we had. I'm thinking in terms of his book of short stories, if I can recall the name right now, it's *Lost in the Funhouse*, that was the important one, *Lost in the Funhouse*, that was a very important book for me. And then *Chimera*, obviously, that's Scheherazade told from the perspective of Scheherazade and things like that. He was very important, and the fact that he told me that he loved Machado de Assis, which was, you know, nice, and that *The Floating Opera*, his first novel, had something to do with Machado de Assis. Actually I have read *The Floating Opera* and I do believe there could be a nice comparative study between it and Machado de Assis — at the time, he was talking more about Borges, and a little bit later, more about García Márquez. And I enjoyed very much his three articles on postmodernism. He was perhaps the first person…

RICHARD KING: 'The Literature of Exhaustion'.

SILVIANO SANTIAGO: 'The Literature of Exhaustion', that was what I was talking about earlier. Imprisoned forms, perhaps, is a little bit like the 'literature of exhaustion', you know, and that was extremely important in my conception of literature, and also I did my dissertation on André Gide, and so Gide was very important for certain themes in my own life. I have talked a lot and yet not a lot about my capacity for being in one place. I think there is something of *disponibilité Gidienne* there, you know, the sense of contradicting myself — usually I write something and my next text is going to be completely different from the other. It's constant — I remember a sentence by Gide in which he says that 'je suis un être en dialogue' — I think that is very important, that I should not be afraid of saying one thing today and something a little bit different the next day, and trying to have a conversation with myself, and discovering that I'm not made of one single piece. Gide was very important. American authors? When I arrived in the United States, I read a lot, you know: Fitzgerald, we just mentioned Faulkner, Hemingway — were influential authors — obviously Katherine Mansfield, James Joyce, things like that were very important, at different moments. Joyce I liked at a certain moment — Joyce was not *Ulysses*, but the *Portrait* and *Dubliners*. And some authors that perhaps no one talks about any more — there was Rosamond Lehmann, a book called *Dusty Answer* — I enjoyed that very much; it was a very important book, you know. It's very strange the way that you shape your readings, I mean, when you try to be a writer, because suddenly it's a non-important book that you discover or someone says, 'Why don't you read this?' and you read and you discover a lot in that particular book. Obviously, most of Brazilian literature. I discovered, when I was in the United States, Latin American literature. Borges, obviously. Borges is very important to my whole way of thinking, García Márquez not that much. What's his name? — the other one, the Peruvian — Mario Vargas Llosa, no, I don't care for Mario Vargas Llosa, not at all. A certain Octavio Paz I like very much. Certain things of Octavio Paz I just love, and North Americans, usually, I read a lot. I read a lot of the bad American — not bad, I mean, important non-important American literature. At the time, a book like

In Conversation

[Robert Gover's] *One Hundred Dollar Misunderstanding* was a fascinating novel. It was about a young boy discovering sex with a black prostitute, and the book was written from the perspective of the young boy, and from the perspective of the prostitute — things like that were not good books, I knew that they were not good books, but they were interesting. One that I read very early, and which then became a classic, was [Horace McCoy's] *They Shoot Horses, Don't They?* I used to read also a lot of Ellery Queen, you know, and people I believe have no importance today. But *The Boy with Green Hair* [by Barbara Haynes] was interesting. I mean, the kind of things that you read and you don't read. I realise now that things like that were important because, you know, they were there. I kept them and I forgot so many other books. I didn't mention just now André Malraux, and I read a lot of him. But I forgot Malraux, so it means that perhaps he didn't have any importance for me. Perhaps. And many others, I'd admit. I have a wide knowledge of French literature, medieval and so on… but I'm saying that I have forgotten, so it means that perhaps they were not so important to me.

ELSE VIEIRA: Bernard, would you like to ask one more question?

BERNARD McGUIRK: Quite the contrary. I feel that I'd just like to close this evening's session. I want to take up a line of possible self-description of Silviano's, or a description of somebody else, because we may have lost any strong sense of whom we're talking about here, in the beauty of the performance and in the intensity of recollection. What I want to do is to pick up the translation of Silviano's novel *Stella Manhattan* — just a few lines in which the narrative broaches the question of performance. 'Bogart. There were times when Humphrey Bogart looked to me like a serious candidate for following in Keaton's footsteps. But Bogart was an aesthete: he had discovered that aloofness is a profitable device for an actor within the Hollywood movie industry. He had discovered how to wield aloofness in art as a form of usury. He cashed in on it. And he drew high returns.' I choose these words because it seems to me that, this evening, we have had an example of the inscription of a character which may or may not be Silviano Santiago (I leave you theorists to decide) but which could hardly be at a more distant remove from the depiction of *this* characterization of Humphrey Bogart. We have seen no aloofness whatsoever. We have heard the confessional. Or have we not? I leave you to decide that, too. But what I will say, to those of you who do not yet know the work of Silviano Santiago, is that *Stella Manhattan* is available in English. There you will find exquisite, moving, and affective treatments of people from his own place, a place which cannot be described in terms of exile or non-exile. In many respects, this colloquium has been about Minas Gerais, about meeting the other, and through the filter of no more splendid a figure of Minas than Silviano. When you read the novel, you will find treatments of the children of Minas, you will find moving treatments of Leila, Aníbal, and Chiquinho. Therefore, it is on a note of mystery, and of invitation, that I ask you to join me in thanking Silviano Santiago.

THE PRISON-HOUSE OF MEMOIRS: SILVIANO SANTIAGO'S *EM LIBERDADE*

K David Jackson

... que par pudieras ser entre mil pares
[...what a peer you might be amongst a thousand peers]
— Orlando Furioso a Don Quijote de la Mancha

Mas julgue-o quem não pode experimentá-lo
[But judge it whoever cannot feel it]
— *Os Lusíadas*

enovelo-me ou libero-me
[I loop myself up or let myself out]
— *Em liberdade*

Simulation and 'De-writing'

In his 1981 fictional work, *Em liberdade,* Silviano Santiago confects counterfeit prison memoirs of renowned author Graciliano Ramos (1892-1953).[1] Ramos's *Memórias do cárcere* (1953) served as Santiago's

---

[1] Memorialism is a strong tradition in modern Brazilian literature. Antecedents include: literary texts, from Machado de Assis *(Memórias póstumas de brás cubas)* to Modernist works (Oswald de Andrade's *Memórias sentimentais de João Miramar)* and contemporary prose (Sérgio Sant'Anna's *Confissões de Ralfo)*; historical and political memoirs, such as recent works on early anarchist and communist movements in Brazil (corresponding in part with Graciliano's memoirs of the Vargas 'Estado Novo' ['New State']of 1937-45); and personal or cultural memoirs, exemplified by Pedro Nava's sweeping six-volume series, *Memórias* (1976-).

Why is memorialism a dominant trend in Brazil, even gaining strength in current letters, while it is weakly represented in Spanish American literature? One theory would be the 'search for identity' that has especially characterized Brazilian civilization since colonial times, expressed in the phrase of historian Stuart Schwartz, 'Who Are We?'. The memoir could be related in this context to the tradition of colonial chronicles of discovery or description. For more than two centuries these descriptive essays directed the narrative voice toward a single absent and distant centre, which was the Portuguese king and court, thus supporting a strong literary tradition joining the epistle, almost in the form of a travel diary, to the descriptive essay.

Alfredo Bosi (1977: 470-78) discusses the memoir in the context of contemporary psychological or intimist literature, whose model is

model to exemplify in contemporary Brazilian prose one of the most prominent currents of the postmodern aesthetic, the reproduction of the real through simulation.[2] The aesthetic of simulation, whose principles Jean Baudrillard describes as the signs of ritual, excess, and equivalence, provides one of the most accessible critical approaches to Santiago's postmodernist strategy, which could be termed the 'de-writing' (implying borrowing or cannibalization) of a noted memoir.[3] As a simulacrum, Santiago's fiction is built first of all on the interplay of language, memory, and history as found in Graciliano's prison memoirs: *Em liberdade* questions the relationship of history and fiction, of speech and language, of thought and reality. The restraints and limits set on literary language by Santiago — the challenge to composition that 'imprisons' the memoir — are inherent to the act of simulation, where the linguistic

---

nineteenth-century interior realism (Chekhov, Machado de Assis, Eça de Queirós, etc.). The psychological dimension tends to interiorize the chronicle, which treats themes of childhood and education as dramas of social consciousness or private desire and emotion. While writers such as Cyro dos Anjos used the classical rhetorical devices of the memoir, producing elegant prose, reliance by others on the interior monologue indicates a passage from psychological to metaphorical and metaphysical prose, while still maintaining the structure of the memoir, as exemplified in works of Osman Lins, Autran Dourado, and Clarice Lispector.

[2] Following Jean Baudrillard's analysis, writing as simulation produces hyperrealism and the joy of an excess of meaning: '[A] thrill of vertiginous and phony exactitude, of alienation and of magnification, of distortion in scale, of excessive transparency all at the same time' (1983: 50). Secondly, simulation is both ritual and illusion. Reality is ritualized as 'a striking resemblance of itself' (1983: 45), while language constructed on other language produces the illusion of referentiality: 'the metalinguistic illusion duplicates and completes the referential illusion' (1983: 148). Thirdly, for Baudrillard the art of simulation is capable of representing a 'social microcosm' (1983: 23), thus attributing to the text the status of a critical consciousness.

[3] Derived from early modernist practices, the procedure at work, described in terms of Gregory Ulmer's essay on the 'lessons of the modernist revolution in representation' (1983: 87), can be traced to the primacy of geometrical fragmentation in techniques of collage and mime:

> The deconstruction is accomplished in fact by borrowing the very terms used by the host work itself [...] and remotivating them, detaching them [...] from one conceptual set or semantic field and reattaching them to another. (Ulmer 1983: 93)

In Conversation

sign functions through an oxymoron of confined freedom (the latitude to produce an 'exact' copy) that, on a more abstract level, parallels the author's problematization of mimesis: '[the] sign is free only to produce the signs of equivalence' (Baudrillard 1983: 86). Simulation ostensibly binds the imagination to the limits of Graciliano's inimitable style and perspective, which paradoxically become the subject of imitation, while equivalence suggests linguistic ambiguity and conceptual repetition.

Assuming a postmodern stance,[4] Santiago's work exploits illusions of equivalence and verisimilitude among several carefully constructed yet 'artificial' conceptual or semantic areas, thereby confusing testimony with invention, matrix with sequel, authenticity with illegitimacy, host with parasite, convention with counterfeit, and narration with simulation. *Em liberdade* affirms the ambiguity and even reversibility of these categories by reproducing Graciliano Ramos's voice in a narrative that purports to be a recuperation of the master's yet unrevealed memoirs of Brazilian life in the late 1930s while manoeuvring within a prison-house of restrictive forms and frames that challenge the writer to act through disguise and duplicity in the role of artist and performer, the absent eminence behind the text. Santiago's counterfeit or false memoirs of Graciliano Ramos free the pseudo-narrator from a literal prison-house, only to lead him, along with his postmodern readers, into other prison-houses of language and of genre — respectively, Graciliano's characteristic style and the nature of the historical memoir. Working within the limitations of chosen linguistic and generic models, Santiago's diary amounts to a portrait of the postmodern writer as escape artist.

Fiction and Confection

In his prison memoirs, Graciliano Ramos recalls the mysterious, threatening telephone call at the beginning of 1936 that would interrupt his life, culminating on the 3rd of March with his arrest by an army lieutenant and long peregrination from the headquarters of the 20th

---

[4] Sources providing a view of the postmodern aesthetic in Brazilian literature and culture include the special issue of the *Revista do Brasil: literatura anos 80* 2, 5 [1986]) edited by Heloisa Buarque de Hollanda, Flora Sussekind's *Literatura e vida literária* (Rio de Janeiro: Zahar, 1985), Rodolfo Franconi's *Erotismo e poder na ficção brasileira dos Anos 80* (Dissertation: Vanderbilt University, 1987), *Cultura brasileira: tradição/contradição* (Rio de Janeiro: Zahar/Funarte, 1987), and essays by José Miguel Wisnik and others.

Battalion in Alagoas to the prison colony on Ilha Grande, near Rio de Janeiro: 'I began to perceive that my stupid *petit-bourgeois* prerogatives were going to come to an end, or had already done so' (1: 22).[5] The interrelationship between fiction and confession in this and other works by Graciliano Ramos has been well documented in critical interpretations:

> Fiction and confession are thus, in the works of Graciliano Ramos, linked by a bridge which gives them continuity and solidarity. (Cândido 1956: 81)

As Cândido observes (1956: 75), literature is both a form of resistance and a source of equilibrium against the disorder Graciliano perceives in social constrictions and personal experience. Scepticism and negation in the portrayal of experience further conceal a primary or primitive current that rejects all social conventions and motivation: 'What am I but a savage, lightly polished, with a thin layer of varnish on the outside?' (Cândido 1956: 23). Memoirs are in this sense perhaps his greatest works of fiction, rejecting the values and norms of society while unifying the contradictory impulses of his world view:

> Hence the importance of *Memórias do cárcere*, in which the man and the writer of fiction come together, and the pessimism of one is completed by the participatory solidarity of the other. (Cândido 1956: 81)

The prison memoirs, begun in 1947, lacked only the final chapter at the time of the author's death in 1953, as testified in a postscript by his son Ricardo Ramos. Having noticed over a period of time his father's apparent reluctance to finish the memoirs, he asked what the nature of the last chapter would be. Graciliano replied, 'Sensations of freedom' (2: 306). The missing final chapter forms the nucleus of Santiago's fictional work, *Em liberdade* (1981), whose introductory materials recapitulate the above information and identify the text as Graciliano's 'lost' manuscript, a diary covering his first two months and 13 days of liberty, from 13 January to 26 March 1937.

---

[5] The same quotation, but without the adjective 'bêstas', is repeated in the 'editor's' note to *Em liberdade* (11).

In Conversation

Silviano Santiago

Postmodern 'grands récits': Imprisoned Memoirs

This essay explores interpretations of *Em liberdade* as ritual and illusion, departing from theories of postmodern culture put forth by Arthur Kroker and David Cook, according to which Santiago's work can be said to construct, necessarily within a negative dimension, one of the 'grands récits' of the age of a new primitivism:

> We're living through a great story — an historical moment of implosion, cancellation and reversal; that [...] traces a great arc of reversal, connecting again to an almost mythic sense of primitivism as the primal scene of technological society. (Kroker and Cook 1988: 15)

Primitivism is centred in Santiago's text in an historical retrogression linked by Kroker and Cook to a will to self-liquidation, itself congruent with the pessimism and scepticism of Graciliano's memoirs: '[t]he governing logic of technological society is *the hyper-atrophication of emotional functions and the hyper-exteriorization of the mind*' (Kroker and Cook 1988: 15). Another primitivist vein of the postmodern in the work, set forth in an essay by Santiago entitled 'The Permanence of the Discourse of Tradition in Modernism', is represented by the location and (re)production of a permanent discourse of tradition within modernism's aesthetic of transgression and destruction (Santiago 1987: 115). In this case, the historical memoir or confession serves as a primary model underlying the regressive simplicity of the modern primitive. Yet a third level of primitivist reading, suggested by the same essay, can be found in the utopian and anti-normative orientation of Graciliano's memoirs: an indigenous primitivism, the 'saber selvagem' emanating from the 'criminally' different, recapitulating the language of Oswald de Andrade's radical 'Manifesto Antropófago' ['Anthropophagous Manifesto'], is posited as the Carib and cannibal rebellion against concepts of an imported European and alien culture (Santiago 1987: 127-8). Santiago's memoir is constructed, as a consequence, not on the apparent tradition of confession but rather through postmodern confection using ingredients of primitivism and simulation. The present analysis will carry Santiago's careful use of simulation into the field of metaphor, as developed in Hayden White's 'visual icons', while allying Brazilian primitivist thought with Michel Serre's illuminating work on parasites. Santiago's 'magical escape' from a self-imposed prison-house of writing,

30

itself a simulation, will be viewed through the conversion of history and language into myth and the formal exploitation of contradictions and self-conscious play in neo-baroque antitheses.[6]

Two Brazilian Prison-Houses

Fredric Jameson's *The Prison-House of Language* argues against the 'attachment to the essentially cryptographic nature of reality' (Jameson 1972: 142), as seen in Lévi-Strauss, and examines critically the notion of the predominance of language over history in modern formalist thought. The critique could well accuse Santiago's self-conscious and self-referential memoir on several points: first, in the epistolary novel, as in the memoir, 'real' events are replaced by literary ones, as the writer calls attention to the activity of writing itself, which becomes the new subject (Jameson 1972: 199-200). Secondly, the binary structure equates perceptions of identity and difference, since 'every linguistic perception holds in its mind at the same time an awareness of its own opposite' (Jameson 1972: 35); and, finally, an alleged defect in the structure itself controls analysis by confining investigation and truth to an infinite, regressive sequence of metalanguages (Jameson 1972: 208). *Em liberdade* constitutes Santiago's fictional 'reply' to these charges by casting the mythical with the existential and reviving neo-baroque play with language and experience.

Linguistic and Generic Models

Throughout the diary, Santiago's narrator constantly reflects on the prison-house of language and genre, which becomes the principal theme

---

[6] According to *The Princeton Encyclopedia of Poetry and Poetics*, baroque style can be viewed as 'an eternal phenomenon, recurrent in all ages' (Preminger 1974: 67). Traits of the baroque revived in Santiago's work include its conceits and wit, 'rhetorical figures such as metaphor, the element of time, the dramatic situation. . . and the implied world view;' especially apparent is 'a tendency to manipulate time and exploit its paradoxes' (Preminger 1974: 67). The illusion of socio-literary identity in Santiago's prose notwithstanding, a central concern is resolution of the problem of opposites (Preminger 1974: 68), linked to an outlook of disequilibrium and disillusionment, represented by freedom and imprisonment, skepticism and commitment, individual and archetypal, etc. The term neo-baroque has been applied to other contemporary Latin American writers.

of the memoir, overshadowing simulation of the socio-political environment of Rio de Janeiro in the 1930s. The narrator becomes aware of a fictional trap in the architecture of his diary: is the writer to be a mere scribe of events, a privileged recipient of history following a score already composed; or can his imagination be called original, shaping an intrinsic language that would invariably transform the diary into a novel that, ironically, no longer narrated the truth? Is there a logic in the narrator's selection of events, or is meaning controlled by chance, embedded in a second or subtext to the diary (*Em liberdade*: 125)? These are questions of writing itself, the suggestion that the memoir, indeed all of writing, is a fiction among fictions, whose true or pre-text, if it exists, is beyond the reach of our 'frightful nothingness'.[7] What might seem initially to be a principle of legitimacy and difference in Santiago's text is revealed by this line of inquiry to be one of identity and convergence. The reader asks 'Who is the true author of the memoir?' and the narrator answers, 'The story writes itself.' By choosing to write in a double prison-house, that is, recasting Graciliano's memoirs as history and story, memoir and fable, event and simulacrum, Santiago provides the reader with the subtext of his own release, as author, from structures of entrapment and enclosure.

Literary hesitations and doubts about the nature of the historical memoir as a genre can be found in the opening chapter of the actual *Memórias do cárcere*: the inevitable and corrosive passage of time; the disproportion between narration and events; possible effects on the lives of living personages who could be misrepresented, etc. On a purely literary level is what Graciliano himself perceives to be a prison-house of the memoir as a genre, its capacity to deform or distort events, and the oppression of literary language through laws of grammar and syntax. Of the first of these, he writes, 'It was repugnant to me to make the book into a kind of novel' (*Memórias* 1: 7), a recognition of the inevitable literariness of the memoir that converts history into fiction through the act of writing. Graciliano addresses the problem of language in what could be taken as a statement of the rules of the game for his future textual double: 'we began oppressed by syntax and ended up (*Memórias*

---

[7] '[C]ar j'entrai tout à coup dans un néant affreux,' writes Santiago's narrator, quoting 'a passage from Montesquieu's *Lettres Persanes*', while perhaps considering himself to be 'a Persian from the state of Alagoas dressed as a cannibal from the Caeté tribe in the Rio de Janeiro night' (*Em liberdade*: 58-9). Graciliano suggests in his memoirs that through the difficult act of writing an author may emerge 'slowly from that horrible world of darkness and death' (*Memórias* 1: 9).

1: 8). Liberty is to be found in the narrow ground for manoeuvring within fixed limits: 'No one enjoys total freedom' (*Memórias* 1: 8). The prison memoirs, in their literal and figurative enclosures, embody the principle of neo-baroque literary play that epitomizes Santiago's textual labyrinth.

Yet another germ of the conceptual play in the contemporary text is expressed by Graciliano in his unexpected baroque approximation of the notions of prison, pleasure, and freedom: 'At that moment the idea of prison gave me near pleasure: I saw there a *beginning* of freedom' (*Memórias* 1: 19). The confining freedom of prison would exempt Graciliano from the unpleasant bourgeois duties of his office and the horrors of provincial political bureaucracy, while granting him the only time and tranquility possible in which to correct the manuscript of an unpublished novel. In a structural inversion typical of carnivalization, freedom and pleasure come into being through imprisonment. The situation is already a double one of fiction within fiction, approaching a continuum, as Graciliano describes his character's desire to write a novel that could reach beyond the humid, black prison bars that confine him (*Memórias* 1: 19). It is, after all, the act of writing that leads to the atemporal and ahistorical consciousness of freedom. As in a baroque conceit, *Em liberdade* strives for expressive freedom through a structure of limitations and enclosures either inherent to or imposed upon history and writing. The prison-houses of the text, intimate counterparts that make the principle of liberty possible, explore the interplay between historical memoir and fiction in a way that considers both to be paradigms, forms, or patterns that underlie the myth of experience and the art of representation.

History and Myth

In his essay 'The Historical Text as Literary Artifact', Hayden White questions the basis of historical consciousness and writing, in particular the relationship of the historical narrative to literature, by comparing historical documents to literary texts. In his structuralist view, White finds that 'verbal fictions', comparable to the function of myth in literature, form the external models of historical representation:

> Viewed in a purely formal way, a historical narrative is not only a reproduction of the events reported in it, but also a complex of symbols which gives us directions for finding an icon of the structure of those events in our literary tradition. (Whyte 1978: 88)

In Conversation

More than a reproduction of events, the narrative 'complex of symbols' contains the icons of a particular literary tradition that endow the unfamiliar with meaning. The mythic structure, embedded in pure form and language, diverts discursive writing into stories and fictions. To read the prison memoirs of Graciliano Ramos, following White's concept, would be to winnow out the patterns and forms of cultural convention capable of revealing structural icons that are encoded in the memoir as genre. In turn, these icons function as the deep framework for interpreting the structural meaning of socio-political and literary reality.

In 'Narrativa histórica e narrativa ficcional' ['Historical narrative and fictional narrative'], Benedito Nunes further provides a critical basis for assessing the fictional component of historical and scientific narratives, which are themselves interrelated:

> History, the researching and recording of the social facts of civilizations, resorts to general laws that are proper to science and also uses fiction; science can restrict itself to the recording of facts, and fiction, through the novel and drama, reaches (borrowing the Aristotelian remark that poetry is 'more philosophical than history') a level of generality similar to scientific thought... The scientific character attained by historical knowledge does not suppress the narrative basis, which keeps its link with the fictional. (Nunes 1988: 12)

The fictive in the historical, the implications of its narrative bias, is yet another prison-house for the author of memoirs, since writing is considered by White to be alienated from the deeper symbolic truths of language and form.

Verbal icons: the drop of sweat and the key

The episodes of the drop of sweat and the key in *Em liberdade* function as White's verbal icons, quasi-parables of the condition of the symbolic forms underlying writer and written. In a short entry to the diary titled 'Antes do jantar' ['Before dinner'], reminiscent, as is much in Graciliano, of Machado de Assis, the narrator notices that a drop of sweat produced by the intolerable heat of a tropical afternoon has fallen onto the written page:

> An unbearable heat this afternoon. While I was reading a few pages of this diary, waiting for dinner, sweat poured down my face until a drop fell onto the written page. I sat thinking about it and its short

fleeting existence. Unlike the arabesque drawn on the paper by pen and ink, the sweat drop will disappear as soon as I write the final draft of this manuscript. (*Em liberdade*: 99)

The drop of sweat and the page, the liquid and the solid, constitute a microcosm of the antithesis between categories of individual and generic, transitory and conventional: the drop of sweat will evaporate, while the writing will be carried into type, print, multiple editions with neatly formed words. The human dimension of the writer, however, is limited to the drop of sweat and its short, passing existence:

> If all the practitioners of literature thought for a minute about the production line and the book industry, they would allow most of their writings to have the transience of a drop of sweat on the written page, in an afternoon of unbearable heat. (*Em liberdade*: 99)

Such is the prison-house of a writer faced with the dilemma of literary production.

The metaphor of the keys in 'Quarta-feira de cinzas' ['Ash Wednesday'], another entry in the diary, carries the concept of incarceration to the level of societal myth:

> It is not by managing to open the prison doors that one reaches freedom faster. It is by not allowing the nearest people to seem to shut them again. The way out of the prison is not through a corridor with countless similar open doors. All friends are prepared to be jailers: each closes one of the successive doors. This is the tragic and unhappy side of the situation. The problem, for me, was always to see first the key to the prison cell in the hand of the person I was going to talk to. Before the key could be used, I impetuously threw myself against him, grabbing it. I thus avoided the doors I pass through in everyday life being closed. (*Em liberdade*: 145)

The most certain path to liberty, states the narrator, does not lie in getting the prison doors to open or even in the social world, where every person is prepared to become a jailer by shutting each of the doors of being or possibility. Incarceration is the narrator's structural icon of social interchange and history, revealed through the unsuspected use of the keys, far beyond their original and apparent social purpose. The icons of the drop of sweat and the key represent the enigmatic, coded nature of experience, resolved through allegory, and further constitute a defence of the 'prison-house' in face of the challenge posed by Jameson.

Flypaper and the Prison-House of Language

35

In Conversation

Silviano Santiago

The narrator's parable of the flypaper illustrates the revolutionary potential of form against repression. Entering a tavern in suburban Maceió, Santiago's narrator, an upstanding citizen, orders cheap *cachaça* [sugar-cane brandy], to the consternation and hostility of the bartender. A bum at the corner table, however, receives attentive, even obsequious treatment. The narrator becomes aware of the shameful barriers that separate him from society's lower depths. Now defending the bum from the hostile opinions of the bourgeoisie, the narrator notes his uncommon verbal aptitude, his ability to tell rich stories that fill time with the food of his imagination: '…the doughy speech of the bum'.

> Coming close to the vagabond, talking to him, one finds out that he has a rare quality in our society in the process of urbanization: thanks to his rare verbal facility, he can always narrate easily and stylishly, with an aura of someone who has daily contact with the task of fiction. He can spend hours filling time with imagination, stuffing it full with pleasure, so that the listener is unaware of time passing. This is the means he has to grip the public and lessen the bitterness of night-time loneliness. (*Em liberdade*: 75)

The narrator is entranced by the directness of the bum's critical vision, the existential perceptiveness of his marginality, and becomes trapped like a fly or mosquito on his inverted literary medium, flypaper:

> The oozing talk of the vagabond (always a cause of nausea) is oozy because it has the gel of glue and sugar. His narratives are like flypaper, on which the heedless insect falls and from where it can no longer spread its wings.
> How many nights I was glued to paper! (*Em liberdade*: 75)

Graciliano's own explanation of his uncompromised freedom of observation and description in the prison memoirs can be related to the bum's irresistible storytelling and social marginality:

> Having performed several tasks, I have forgotten them all and thus can move without any embarrassment. Methods do not grab me, nothing forces me to slow scrutiny. On the other hand, I do not force myself to reduce a panorama, to subject it to regular dimensions, complying with the paginator and the tram-passenger's timetable. I can walk to the right and to the left like a vagabond, concentrate on long stops, skip places of no interest, stroll, run,

return to familiar places. I shall omit essential knowledge or mention it in passing, as if I saw it through small lenses; I shall amplify trivia, I shall repeat them to exhaustion, if I find this convenient. (*Memórias* 1: 9-10)

The telling of pleasurable stories, the flypaper narratives of a thousand and one nights, is capable of inverting the prison-house of social difference through the introduction of a parasitical metaphor.

'Scriptophagia': Host/Guest, Eater/Eaten

In the essay 'The Critic as Host', J. Hillis Miller (1977) considers the implications of M. H. Abrams' statement that 'any history which relies on written texts becomes an impossibility'. Miller addresses questions of textual identity and difference in the context of historical referents by using the critical metaphor of host and parasite. Santiago's narrator touches on the same theme by defining the reader as a parasite on the memoir, a voyeur who invades 'real' action with his imagination:

> Without noticing it, the listener already wriggles parasitically into the real action, forgetting that, for him, it is only imaginary. We are all *voyeurs* of other people's conquests, *envious*, or else bodies on the stage, proud, for other *voyeurs*. If we don't see the canvas painted with the other's words, it is because we are narrating the action (narrating is more important than experiencing). (*Em liberdade*: 30)

If, as in Brazilian anthropophagy, the cannibal/narrator can be defined only in relation to his supposed opposite, a victim/reader who will serve as his food, the primary text may already support an uncanny alien meaning as a necessary and dangerous counterpart, its difference.[8] The parasitical relationship is described by Miller as one of double antithesis:

> 'Para' is an 'uncanny' double antithetical prefix signifying at once proximity and distance, similarity and difference, interiority and exteriority, something at once inside a domestic economy and outside it, something simultaneously this side of the boundary line, threshold, or margin, and at the same time beyond it, equivalent in status and at the same time secondary or subsidiary, submissive, as

---

[8] This is the concept of difference developed by Jacques Derrida in *L'écriture et la différence* (Paris: Éditions du Seuil, 1967).

of guest to host, slave to master. (Miller 1977: 441)

Following his argument, the dynamic of both cannibal and parasite would question boundaries and limits, suggesting their interpenetration. The apparent polarity of the relationship host/guest, or eater/eaten, with its superimposition of intimate kinship and ritual enmity, is transmuted into the complexity and openness of reciprocal obligation, in which one element fulfils the role of the other. If in the world of literature the text becomes a food needed by each, thus establishing an interplay of asymmetrical relationships, in the Brazilian context writer and reader can equally and interchangeably be identified as 'escritófagos', or cannibals of the written word.

The relevance of the cannibal model to Santiago's memoir can be further intensified by returning to the bum and the key in the light of Michel Serres' work, *The Parasite*. The bum's 'doughy speech' is both a food and a medium of exchange, placed by social convention outside the reach of hosts or bourgeois diners. Following Serres, the bum pays for his food with words:

> The parasite is invited to the table d'hôte; in return, he must regale the other diners with his stories and his mirth. To be exact, he exchanges good talk for good food; he buys his dinner, paying for it in words. It is the oldest profession in the world. (Serres 1982: 34)

The parasite thereby invents something new by changing the order of things. The bum/parasite not only exchanges his voice for matter (sound for solid) but also speaks in a logic previously considered irrational and ungovernable. Dependent on the host's table for trapping his food with words, the bum's revenge is the flypaper of his irresistible tales. As Serres observes, 'Each society allows a linguistic specie that can be exchanged advantageously for food. Influential and powerful groups are able to diffuse a forced lexicon in that way' (Serres 1983: 34). Like lexical and economic relationships, language and specie are subject to the laws of the prison-house.

Turning to the case of the key, the narrator exhausts himself by seeking to conquer the social and existential barriers imposed by those who wield it through his copious use of conventional language:

> This hurdle-race made me an agile word athlete... I would plunge into conversation with the ease of a lawyer from the state of Bahia. (*Em liberdade*: 146)

Words are the specie through which the prisoner/parasite attempts to re-enter the world of social exchange, as he puts it, with the tactics of a general but avoiding the word 'cadeia' ['jail'] at all costs.

> I became wordy, chatty and curious about each and every subject coming from my interlocutor. I gained ground, advanced, carried the battle to its end, I saw myself victorious. A general would envy my tactics for conquering the adversary in so-called social life. (*Em liberdade*: 146)

But because the prisoner lacks the bum's saving indifference, he therefore cannot find the free language he seeks. Santiago's postmodern narrative in this sense expresses both the alienation of the different and the convention of imitation.

For a literary author, Miller considers the parasitic system by which the host becomes the food to argue in favour of the 'hyperbolic exuberance' of a given text or language taken to its limits.

> [Deconstructive strategy] provides a model for the relation of critic to critic, for the incoherence within a single critic's language, for the asymmetrical relation of critical text to poem, for the incoherence within any single literary text, and for the skewed relation of a poem to its predecessors. (Miller 1977: 444)

The weight of the prison-house of language can thereby be reduced or disguised, he asserts, by its translation into an expansive universe, through the mutual reversibility of roles, and by the metamorphosis of historical description into myth.

> The complexity and equivocal richness, my discussion of 'parasite' implies, resides in part in the fact that there is no conceptual expression without figure, and no intertwining of concept and figure without an implied story, narrative, or myth, in this case the story of the alien guest in the home. (Miller 1977: 443)

Neo-Baroque Sleight of Hand

Santiago places Graciliano's memoirs within an elaborate neo-baroque frame whose counterfeit purpose, while transparent to the reader, is to affirm the text's legitimacy through a carefully prepared provenance. The 'editor' of *Em liberdade*, who has come into possession of the manuscript, states the case for its authenticity: written by Graciliano in 1946, it was

In Conversation

confided to a friend to be kept until twenty-five years after the author's death; in 1952 the author decided to burn the memoir and so instructed his friend, who lied in saying that he had carried out the request. Because of the editor's acquaintance and long conversations with the unnamed friend, upon the latter's death in 1965 his widow, having found the editor's address on top of the manuscript, mailed it to his teaching post at Rutgers University.

The editor affirms the impeccable credentials of his dossier: he has guarded the manuscript in secret another fifteen years; he has obeyed the author's twenty-five year restriction before publication; he has even after a fashion 'solicited' the originals from the author, who never denied other manuscripts to an editor; he has not revealed the friend's name; and he has accepted responsibility for the consequences of his act. Yet even within the legalistic presentation of facts, dates, and events, the editor hits upon uncanny literary parallels that suggest deceptive, recurring patterns or rhythms: the friend whose lie saved the memoir is compared to the story of Max Brod and the works of Kafka; the editor himself is at work on a presumably unpublished chapter of Gide's *The Counterfeiters*. Perhaps the editor has confused his editing of a true counterfeit with the interlacing of footnotes in the Brazilian manuscript that identify marginal notations, erasures, arrows, parentheses, quotations, additions in red ink, or the use of a different kind of paper. As if to define mimesis as sincere deception, the editor reminds the reader that his Graciliano considered the manuscript at hand, his final chapter, to be the contrary of what a reader habituated to prison memoirs was prepared to accept: 'I shall not give you the book you demand from me. I shall give you in exchange what you don't want. [...] I am working on your disappointment. It is the raw material of this diary' (*Em liberdade*: 128).[9]

---

[9] While toying within the prison-house of textual criticism, the complex frame of *Em liberdade* at the same time firmly places the memoir in a central tradition of Western fiction that questions the nature of authorship and writing. In the prologue to the *Ingenioso Hidalgo Don Quijote de la Mancha* (1605), the narrator exploits mimesis: 'in [the Natural Order] each thing engenders its like'. Pronouncing himself devoid of the talent necessary to write the discreet and intelligent book of his dreams, the author is reduced to dissimulation of tradition: 'But I, though I seem a father, am step-father of Don Quixote, and I don't want to go with the flow of usage…' The play between author, narrator and text — where the appearance of truth coexists with the disguising of fiction — is a practice firmly established in Portuguese literature from the *cantigas de*

Recurring Rhythms: Memoir and Myth

The historical memoir can be displaced by the establishment of a rhythm underlying the recurrence of events that casts the diary into literature and myth. This rhythm is achieved in Santiago's diary by the introduction of a countertheme from colonial Brazilian history that also expresses the metaphor host/guest and the aesthetic of simulation. In early March, 1937, the narrator of *Em liberdade* has a dream, presumably triggered by too much champagne and whisky, that draws him back to 1789. The dream's main character is also a prisoner writing a diary, none other than the poet and rebel Cláudio Manuel da Costa (1729-89) of the *Inconfidência*.[10] For lack of paper the character writes on a wooden table,

---

amigo, where the voice of a young maiden flows from a masculine pen. In Renaissance prose, the *Prymera parte da cronica do emperador Clarimundo donde os Reys de Portugal descendem* [*First part of the Chronicle of the Emperor Clarimund whence descend the Kings of Portugal*] (1522), a chivalric novel by humanist João de Barros, presents itself as being a translation of a previously existent Hungarian manuscript that relates the life of a fictitious 'Emperor Clarimundo', who in turn is the false father of Count Henry of Burgundy, who is the true father of D. Afonso Henriques, the first king of Portugal. This fiction did not pretend to deceive its cultured readers; its purpose was to create a textual mythology capable of transforming history into legend, transfiguring royal characters into heroes of magical adventures of chivalric novels. Disguised in verisimilitude, the author of this 'translation' made use of fiction in order to candidate himself to the post of royal historiographer, which he became as author of the *Decades* of Asia, texts which themselves relate the truth of distant lands unknown to the author: *Asia de Joam de Barros dos fectos que os Portugueses fizeram no descobrimento e conquista dos mares e terras do Oriente* [*Asia of Joam de Barros of the deeds of the Portuguese in the discovery and conquest of seas and lands of the Orient*] (1552). To the extent that the chronicle approximates fictional narrative to contemporary history, the *Decades*, like the memoir in question, 'translated' distant historical reality, veiled by time and the seas, incorporating it into the problematics of European narrative traditions. Portuguese historiography took on mythological proportions.

[10] Cláudio Manuel da Costa (1729-89), Brazil's greatest neo-classical poet, who studied Law in Coimbra (*Obras* 1768; *Obras poéticas*, ed. João Ribeiro [Rio de Janeiro: Garnier, 1903]), was one of the *árcades mineiros* of Vila Rica. Arrested and interrogated during the *Inconfidência*, he was found dead in his jail cell. Santiago's text exploits Costa's personal and

and his desire to write is further frustrated because the same words keep repeating. The narrator recognizes that the character is in truth himself, Graciliano, writing Cláudio's diary of persecution during the colonial *Inconfidência* [Uprising].

This realization shocks the narrator out of his stupor, and he decides to confront the dream by marshalling his forces to produce a story of significance and imagination.

> I write these trivialities that afflict me and might afflict the reader.
>
> Why don't I write something more meaningful? Why don't I face the dream, as a bull, and construct with it a spectacle named short story? (*Em liberdade*: 202-3)

He gathers up and examines all the data at hand about the rebellion of Vila Rica and begins to deconstruct the existing history of the event, in which he recognizes the mythical glorification of a martyr, and returns to a literary examination of the memoir and the poet:

> I want to rethink, without prejudice, all the plot woven by what we call historical tradition… I shall propose, with the short story, a new interpretation of man's action, trying to figure out the reasoning and the motivation underlying acts and words. The work of imagination enters at this moment. (*Em liberdade*: 206)

The narrator's obsession with the writing of Cláudio's story is comparable to the 'thermal excitement' (Serres 1982: 190) brought about by Serres' parasite, who produces fluctuations in systems and messages and places human actions and relations in a different light:

> The parasite is an exciter. Far from transforming a system changing its nature, its form, its elements, its relations and its pathways… the parasite makes it change states differentially. . . The parasite intervenes, enters the system as an element of fluctuation. [It] changes its energetic state. (Serres 1982: 191)

Related to fluctuation and continuum is the narrator's revised description of double memoirs: 'writing your life as if it were mine, writing my life as if it were yours' (*Em liberdade*: 209). The narrator's

---

historical affinities, as author and sacrificed member of a national liberation movement, with Graciliano Ramos's prison memoirs of some 150 years later.

rethinking of historical tradition recapitulates Santiago's own repetition of the prison memoir by examining the relationship of its internal antitheses: history/story, fact/myth, etc. The historical memoir is thereby revisited and validated as dream or story of multiple meanings.

Ghost writer/writer ghost

Em liberdade is (re)constructed as an individual literary memoir of collective language, generic experience, and literary form: 'Graciliano redige, mas quem escreve é Cláudio' (Serres 1982: 234). If Graciliano's prison memoirs, in their unmistakable 'dry and concise' style, were the work not of a ghost writer but a writer ghost, the reader could better recognize the antithetical nature of the deceptive question posed by Santiago's text: 'Who is the writer of *Em liberdade*?' Claudio's text resonates in Graciliano's prison memoirs, and, by projection, in Santiago's contemporary simulation, making all three moments participants in a Brazilian paradigm of socio-literary crime and punishment. Story, myth, and archetype are restored as shaping forces of the historical memoir.

Through a neo-baroque play of forms, Santiago's fiction revives yet another, postmodern dimension of the memoir: the status of art, or art object. Through their rich artistic imaginations, both Cláudio Manual da Costa and Graciliano Ramos would be capable of envisioning a utopia of liberty in the national prison-house of slave labour and social convention. Their superimposed memoirs of imprisonment or persecution as an art of writing, filtered through the recurring metaphor of national experience in the 1960s and '70s, recapitulate an open-ended and paradoxical apprenticeship of individual craft to demanding models. Through an art of imitation, Silviano Santiago encounters a carefully constructed freedom in the mythical forms of writing itself, one of the possible answers to the prison-houses of literature and experience.

43

In Conversation

REFERENCES

Baudrillard, Jean. *Simulations*, tr. Paul Foss, Paul Patton and Philip Beitchman (New York: Semiotext(e), 1983).

Bosi, Alfredo. *História concisa da literatura brasileira* (2nd ed.; São Paulo: Cultrix, 1977).

Cândido, Antônio. *Ficção e confissão* (Rio de Janeiro: José Olympio, 1956).

Jameson, Fredric. *The Prison-House of Language: a Critical Account of Structuralism and Russian Formalism* (Princeton: Princeton University Press, 1972).

Kroker, Arthur and David Cook. *The Postmodern Scene: Excremental Culture and Hyper-Aesthetics* (2nd. ed.; New York: St. Martin's Press, 1988).

Lyotard, Jean-François. *La condition postmoderne* (Paris: Minuit, 1979).

Miller, J. Hillis. 'The Critic as Host', *Critical Inquiry* 3 (1977), 439-47.

Nava, Pedro. *Memórias* (6 vols.; Rio de Janeiro: Olympio, 1976-).

Nunes, Benedito. 'Narrativa histórica e narrativa ficcional', in *Narrativa: ficção e história.*, ed. Dirce Côrtes Riedel (Rio de Janeiro: Imago, 1988), 9-22.

Preminger, Alex (ed.). *The Princeton Encyclopedia of Poetry and Poetics* (Princeton: Princeton Univesity Press, 1974).

Ramos, Graciliano. *Memórias do cárcere* (2 vols; 5th ed.; São Paulo: Martins, 1965).

Revista do Brasil: literatura anos 80. 2, 5 (1986).

Santiago, Silviano. 'Permanência do discurso da tradição no modernismo', *Cultura brasileira: tradição contradição* (Rio de Janeiro: Zahar, 1987), 111-45.

Santiago, Silviano. 'Para além da história social.', in *Narrativa: ficção e história*, ed. Dirce Côrtes Riedel (Rio de Janeiro: Imago, 1988), 241-56.

Serres, Michel. *The Parasite*, tr. Lawrence R. Schehr (Baltimore and London: Johns Hopkins University Press, 1982).

Ulmer, Gregory L. 'The Object of Post-Criticism', in *The Anti-Aesthetic: Essays on Postmodern Culture*, ed. Hal Foster (Port Townsend, Washington: Bay Press, 1983), 83-110.

White, Hayden. *Tropics of Discourse* (Baltimore: Johns Hopkins University Press, 1978).

SILVIANO SANTIAGO: DOUBLE STILETTO
Wander Melo Miranda

Initial contact with Silviano Santiago's critical work surprises and confuses the reader. How can one remain indifferent, despite one's institutionalized convictions, when confronted by thoughts which unfold multifaceted, apparently fragmentary and unfinished, across a broad spectrum which, however, constitutes our field of cultural and literary enquiry?

Nothing escapes a scrutinising gaze that seeks to encompass the relations and meanings of the Brazilian cultural condition: from Pero Vaz de Caminha's stratagem-letter to the domination-baptism of José de Alencar's Poti and to the doubtful seed-word of Padre Antônio Vieira's sermons; from the mistakes of a culture undermined by a bachelor mentality and Jesuit morality to the contradictions of the modernist writer; from the perpetuation of symbolic possessions of blood and clan in Carlos Drummond de Andrade's memory to Graciliano Ramos's lucid and uncompromising X-ray of Brazilian reality; from the *tropicalista* movement of the marginal literature of the seventies to the autobiography of the post-'64 generation; and lastly, to the relevant reflection on cultural dependence and the concept of 'the universal' in Latin American, especially Brazilian, literature.

To this wide range of criticism and theoretical reflection, Santiago's artistic production must be added, the latter standing as a supplement to what was unfinished in the former. Both of them work simultaneously or in parallel towards one long essay — in the sense of writing which does and redoes itself so as to probe the many possibilities available in the wording of the text to contemporary dialogue between critical production and literary creation. In order to grasp the scope of this 'subject-in-transit' (a metaphor borrowed from Flora Süssekind [1988]), it is enough to remember the essay-cum-fiction *Em liberdade* [*In Liberty*] (1981) and *Stella Manhattan* (1985), besides the book of short stories *O banquete* [*The Banquet*] (1970), in which it is already possible to find the illuminating interface between criticism and artistic production.

On rereading, Santiago's work emerges as a well-organized canvas, not only of the critic's intentions and interpretations, but also of the links between his work and the best Brazilian thinking of the last few decades. In order to grasp this, it is necessary to approach Santiago's critical thinking as a deconstruction of the Brazilian social and cultural imaginary, highlighting the relation between the intellectual and power, and to attend to its marked comparative bias towards Brazilian culture.

Silviano Santiago

In Conversation

Short-circuit of words in the tropics

In 'Análise e Interpretação' ['Analysis and Interpretation'], the closing essay in *Uma literatura nos trópicos* [*A Literature in the Tropics*] (Santiago 1978b: 191-207), Santiago approaches the work of French scholars from the sixties and seventies, and makes the theoretical guidelines underlying the readings carried out in his book more explicit and systematic. The outlining of the theoretical framework — in which other studies by the author are to be found, in varying degrees — covers the review of the fundamental assumptions of structuralism, through the conceptual post-structuralist system represented by the thinking of Michel Foucault, Gilles Deleuze and, especially, Jacques Derrida.

The system of textual analysis of structuralist activity derived from the teachings of Lévi-Strauss, Propp and the early Barthes is questioned, since it would reduce itself to a 'formal bi-dimensionalism', determined, roughly speaking, by the stages of dismantling and rebuilding the object and by the consequent addition to it of the 'intelligible'. The result would be a whole which is closed, in which the 'game and the relation exhausted themselves in the centring resulting from totalitarian reconstitution' (Santiago 1978b: 197), which is responsible for the reduction of the difference from it and by the abolition of the propelling force contained in the texts analysed.

The limits of this theoretical field are overcome when the operational concept of *différance* is introduced, in which the play and the relation are recovered as structuring elements and the concept of intertextuality is emphasized:

> Through the difference one begins to think of the occurrence of the articulation of one text over others. They are no longer considered as texts in isolation, or as belonging to a single model of the same, but as differentiating themselves in repetition, as a dialogue between the same and the Other. The issue of 'subject' is raised again (of the 'author', in literary terms), since there is not a clear and resounding origin to be sought in the process of explaining the text, which would also be the origin of the truth of this text and which becomes clear in the process of literary analysis. A confusing moment must be recognized — confusion of writings — since the texts only speak significantly through insertion. (Santiago 1978b: 199)

In the wake of Derrida's deconstruction of western metaphysics and Deleuze's inversion of Platonism, this formulation contrasts with the previous theoretical model and opens the way for interpretation, seen as an infinite, incomplete, polysemic and anti-totalitarian task. It is not the 'semiological' reduction of the object(s), but the decentring of their structure, the getting away from totalizing model-building, the epistemological deconstruction of thier 'transcendental meaning' and opening up to the contradictory and unceasing play of meanings. The written text, according to the criticism of Platonic phonocentrism by Derrida, must wander helplessly, without the presence of the father to correct, improve or guide the words of the child-text.

The initial adoption of this theoretical perspective allows Santiago to escape both a strictly formalist approach to literary texts as well as a consideration of them from the point of view of sociologizing concepts. The effectiveness of the position he adopts is made clearer in his dealings with the relations between subject and discourse, subject and social-cultural-political organization, a kind of constant that weaves through the many investigations of literature and culture in general.

A clear example is the reading of Carlos Drummond de Andrade, in the book of the same name, where the rigour of method operates in the service of what is declared in the preface to *Uma Literatura nos trópicos* about the role of the interpreter. He is supposed to enrich the work with 'a layer of complementary meaning' so that the reader 'finds fewer intuitive trampolines for the reading jump' (Santiago 1978b: 10), although the interpreter himself still competes creatively with the poet, as the producer of text that he is, too. The reading of Drummond's work begins with a confrontation between the memoir-style autobiographical poems of *Boitempo* and the remainder of the author's poetry. It seeks to detect how Drummond's subject, ideologically configured, is inserted in language in order to be recognized as belonging to a certain social class, the values of which it approves and for which it becomes a kind of guardian.

Santiago states that although the poet, like a new Robinson Crusoe, has created on the reading-island a space of individual freedom independent and far from the family space, he is forced to return by the hand of the Father, in a settlement where the father must perpetuate the symbolic goods of blood and clan. In order to affirm himself as a conscious and mature adult, the son-poet must not only overcome the fear of this unequal struggle, but, above all, try to reduce the heredity of the past to a 'tabula rasa', on which may be written the 'independent word free from land and blood, free from any trace of debt from its origin' (Santiago 1976: 103). A founder of being, circulating intransitively through the poem, the word, he states, is a debt to the Father, from whom he borrows it, and it operates as a 'credit' to the poem, which writes itself, erasing and, at the same time, encompassing all traces of the beginning-word, to give way to 'another identical being, that is *to generate the same in difference'* (Santiago 1976: 106).

The 'logic of dependence' that Drummond's poetry expresses, through the movement of the poet's oscillation between the murder of the father and the attempt to recover the 'origin' as the value of values, goes beyond the specific case of one word and one author, and becomes the object of Santiago's critical thinking, when he finds it spread like the logic of domination, in a variety of discourse structures at crucial moments of Brazilian culture.

In 'A Palavra de Deus' ['The Word of God'] (Santiago 1970a), the seminal study related to the Author's interests, the strategic paths of colonization and catechism are analysed through the reading of the letter of Pero Vaz de Caminha, of José de Alencar's *Iracema* and a sermon by Padre Antônio Vieira. Colonization and catechism are seen as the imposition of a linguistic and religious code by the colonizer on the colonized — an imposition based, of course, on the abolition of difference with the intention of narcissistically converting the autochthonous element. Or, as is summarized later in 'Porque e Para Que Viaja o Europeu' ['Why and For What the European Travels'], a long critical summary of the mistakes of *Viagem pela irrealidade cotidiana* [*Journey through Daily Reality*] by Umberto Eco:

> the colonization by the preaching of the Faith and of the Empire is a negation of the values of the Other [...] The triple negation of the Other, to be more precise. First: from the social point of view, because the native loses his freedom and becomes the subject of a European crown. Second: he is forced to abandon his religious system (and all it means, economically, socially and politically) and becomes — by the force of catechism — a mere copy of the Europeans. Third: he loses his linguistic identity, gradually expressing himself in a language which is not his own. (Santiago 1989: 192-193)

In these and other texts, in which there is a clear anthropological basis, acquired by the reading of works such as *Tristes Tropiques* [*Sad Tropics*] by Lévi-Strauss, the question of alterity and its impasses, from the beginning of colonization until its more recent developments, reveals itself as dominant, and unfolds in a number of other issues. The most relevant of these is undoubtedly that of the dependent aspect of Brazilian and Spanish-American literature. By analysing it, Santiago places himself, with his own theoretical-methodological peculiarities, in the field of critical thinking which, among us, has approached the problem in greater detail, whether from the relation 'literature and underdevelopment' (Antônio Cândido), whether from the topic of 'misplaced ideas' (Roberto Schwarz), or by the 'dialectic between non-being and being the Other' (Paulo Emilio Sales Gomes).

In the field of comparative literature, a privileged sphere for the dissection of the issue, Santiago shows himself immune to evolutionist concepts and firmly against ethnocentric ones. He shows this by beginning with the provocative title of the essay, 'Eça, Autor de *Madame Bovary*' ['Eça, Author of *Madame Bovary*'] (1970), in *Uma Literatura nos trópicos*, which is complemented by another study in the same book, 'O Entre-Lugar Do Discurso Latino-Americano' ['The In-betweenness of Latin American Discourse'] and by 'Apesar de Dependente, Universal' ['However Dependent, Universal'], in *Vale quanto pesa* [*It is Worth its Weight*] (Santiago 1982).

In the last two, the ideological fallacy which is often wrapped around ideas such as source and influence is dismantled with the reaffirmation of the value of copy *vis à vis* the model. The relation between them is no longer seen as the *cul-de-sac* of dependence and the impossibility of a Latin American cultural identity, but as a process of differentiated repetition in which an attempt is made to insert the autochthonous culture into western culture. This way, through the reversal of values such as 'backwardness' and 'originality', the in-betweenness of the text of the colonized culture which acts on the text of the dominant is affirmed. This is an indispensable movement of concrete evaluation of the universality of the text from the home country.

It is neither flippantly nor randomly, therefore, that the attention of the critic is directed mostly at Brazilian *Modernismo*. As the first joint effort of deprovincialization and cultural updating, it marks with 'anthropophagous' clarity the conflict between the dominated and dominating discourses and inserts in the discussion a great series of issues relative to the problem. Therefore in 'Vale Quanto Pesa (A Ficção Brasileira Modernista)' [It is Worth its Weight: Brazilian Modernist Fiction], 'Fechado para Balanço (60 Anos de Modernismo)' ['Closed for Auditing (60 Years of Modernism')] or 'Permanência do Discurso da Tradição No Modernismo' ['Permanence of the Tradition Discourse in Modernism'], the interpreter joins the literary historian, or better, the 'archaeologist'.

The critical review undertaken by Santiago is not limited to the description of formal achievements, aesthetically revolutionary and libertarian, which occur in works of the period, but seeks to relate them to the process of modernization of Brazilian society: 'Connivance in

In Conversation

authoritarianism, consensus in the cultural project. Hand in hand: politics and art, *Modernismo* and *Estado Novo*' (Santiago 1989: 80). Here is a synthesis of the issue that the previous studies on the subject repressed or passed over unnoticed. In order to discuss it, Santiago begins with a reflection on memorialism — that important strain of modernist production which had hitherto been underestimated (for reasons which are obvious today):

> In our best novels of *Modernismo*, the text of memory feeds the text of fiction, the affective memory of childhood and adolescence sustains the literary make-believe, indicating the importance that the account of the writer's life, family and fellow citizens has in the process of understanding the transformation undergone by the dominant class in Brazil, in the transition from the *Segundo Reinado* [*Second Kingdom*] to the Republic, and from the First to the Second Republic. This importance stems from the fact that he — writer or intellectual, in the widest sense — is an essential part of this power, in that his being is deeply rooted in one of the 'great Brazilian families'. (Santiago 1982: 31)

The memoirs, the autobiographies and the correspondence between the modernists provide material to draw the profile of the intellectuals of the movement and to establish the relations they had with power and the instances of legitimization of their work. In this sense, the contribution of sociological works such as *Intelectuais e classe dirigente no Brasil (1920-1945)* [*Intellectuals and the Ruling Class in Brazil (1920-1945)*] by Sergio Miceli is decisive. Nevertheless, Santiago, unlike Miceli, makes the writer's life story, and experience, flow into the literary work. From this point of view, the writer's political attitude, the quality of his work and his relations to the labour market are thought through, jointly, and with greater precision, in studies like 'Calidoscópio de Questões' ['Kaleidoscope of Questions'] and in 'O Intelectual Modernista Revisitado' ['The Modernist Intellectual Revisited']. This position works as an effective methodological strategy for the stating of issues inherent to Brazilian literary production in the last two decades, inserting it in the field of thought established by the most recent surveys of post-modernity.

Unheimliche library

Caetano Veloso's statement ('I cannot deny what I have read, nor can I forget where I live'), reproduced by Santiago when he studies the work of the *tropicalista* 'superstar', is more than a beautiful phrase deployed just for effect. It summarizes with rare precision the status of the Brazilian cultural producer, or Latin Americans in general, confined to the narrow limits of dependency on the dominant production centres.

The approach of marginal or reflex literatures must deal, therefore, with dependence, which is carried out from a comparative perspective, as Santiago says, through Antônio Cândido, defining the object of study of comparative literature: 'the object must be double, made up as it is of literature generated in different national contexts, but which are, however, analysed through contrast in order to widen both the limited horizon of artistic knowledge, and the critical view of national literatures' (Santiago 1982: 19).

It is not, of course, the mechanistic reduction of the artistic text to the social process from which it comes, nor the evasion of this relation. It is a matter of making it interact, given the fact that the subject-producer moves through the corridor of a library, the books of which, inevitably out of place, will seem to him both strange and familiar — whether due to the fact that they subsume a 'foreign sign' or because they are the constant object of appropriation, digestion, defined by a 'kind of global translation, of pastiche, parody, digression' (Santiago 1978b: 23) and placed in a cultural context marked by something similar to the Freudian *unheimliche*.

The idea of original and copy is fundamental in this process. Presuppositions inherent in this process, such as identification, plagiarism and transgression are discussed through references to the innovatory work of Borges, in so far as it accepts the dominant culture as imprisoning and, at the same time, as an active revolt against this imprisonment. The concept of *prison-form* (sought by Santiago in the poetry of Robert Desnos) is seen as an initial obstacle to the effective action of dependent production; its use enables the reader to set up a dialogue with the model borrowed from the dominant culture: this dialogue ends up revealing the difference established by the copy. From this point of view, the decolonized text of the dominated culture begins to have an unforeseen richness and energy: *'since it contains in itself a representation of the dominant text and a response to this representation at the very level of the plot*; this response becomes the standard for gauging universality, as effective as those already known and accepted' (Santiago 1982: 23).

In this two-way traffic the conceptual break with the primal is brought about by philosophical abstraction, and the self-esteem of the intellectual in the underdeveloped world, as argued by a Marxist-oriented criticism, such as that of Roberto Schwarz. The claims that such a

In Conversation

conceptual break does not 'solve or oppose the relations of effective subordination' (Schwarz 1987: 36), although brilliantly developed by Schwarz, do not hold when the process of deconstruction of the ideas of original and copy, as carried out by Santiago, are analysed carefully, without the mistakes of realist reading. The greatest of these mistakes, undoubtedly, is that of considering the text to be an illustration or symptom of the context.

The initial step is taken, in 'Apesar de Dependente, Universal' and in other essays by the author through the 'archaeological retreat' of the critic towards the origins of the formation of discursive practices, that is, when the impasse of the European holy wars are shifted from their place of origin to the New World. The result of the displacement is seen as the imposition of an ethnocentric cultural standard, which is clear, in the Brazilian case, from the catechism activity of Padre José de Anchieta, who introduces the Indian into a battlefield to which he does not belong, and demands of him the absorption of a strange social, political and economic situation — that of the unity of the church and the constitution of the strong European state.

The conversion of the Indian, at the end of the sixteenth century, dislodges him from his own culture. Thus unclothed of his true otherness and reduced to a simulacrum of the European, he begins to memorize and live a European fiction. The creation of schools, in the same century, reinforces the teaching aspect of the colonising action and the role of memory as a fundamental requisite for this, since foreign history is imposed narcissistically as material for memorising in a process which seeks to reduce different existing civilizations to a single form, to westernize the newly discovered and the strategic imposition of European history as universal history. Later on, the institutionalization of the dominant class as the possessor of a cultural discourse occurs, therefore, via the hierarchical forgetting of the autochthonous or black African values through the preservation of European culture as the only holder of knowledge and truth, as a culture of reference which establishes the hierarchies. The dilemma that permeates its later impasses is established at the setting-up of a 'Brazilian *intelligentsia*'.

The historical and anthropological decentralising achieved by critical enquiry does not occur in the sphere of abstract debate, based as it is on the political and cultural causes of the problem. By making use of anthropological rather than historical discourse in order to fill in the methodological gaps which the latter fails to deal with, Santiago captures what permits us to detect a possible identity for Brazilian cultural production. This occurs precisely because he does not treat as secondary a determining factor of the equation — the place of the intellectual in peripheral cultures — which only the interaction of *both* discourses can locate with greater clarity, effectiveness and adequacy. The intellectual is both explained and destroyed by historical discourse, in so far as he highlights the fact that we live 'a fiction, since they made European history our own story'. The selfsame intellectual, recovered and constituted, although not explained, by anthropology, becomes as a cultural entity an ambivalent in-between, drawn by the borders of the two disciplines, 'since that which is superstition for History makes up the concrete reality of our past' (Santiago 1982: 18).

It is from this position that the critic speaks and manages to unveil the process of disqualifying and hierarchising of the product of the dominated culture. This process begins with the initial simulacrum of the model from the metropolis; it goes through the period in which it begins to be questioned by the copy, however timidly in the nineteenth century; it ends, in *Modernismo*, with the actual overcoming of the copy. The last two cases are illustrated in the studies carried out by the author on the work of José de Alencar and on the literary production of *Modernismo*.

In his writings, José de Alencar enquires into a still fragile escape from the ethnocentric view imposed by the dominant culture, through the recovery of that which is typically Brazilian, seen as the process of *un*repression of the Other. The Indian is taken as the symbol of national affirmation, although he does not fully escape the exotic framing given by the European Romantic model, nor from the 'baptism' that inserts him in a set of moral, ethical and religious values which do not bear on him. In spite of this, the dramatic use of the Indian issue in the scene of the text allows Alencar 'to establish, develop and codify, in writing and thoughtfully, the *new* values that begin to appear anarchically, that is, those that will finally determine the social structure of the country and the hierarchy among its inhabitants' (Santiago 1982: 90).

In order to conclude his proposal, Santiago chooses a path not often used until then by comparative studies; instead of stopping at a survey of 'influences', and the debt of Alencar's text to European ones, he prefers to map out the trails of the latter left in the former by the 'socio-economic values that already made up a certain, heavy and recent tradition' (Santiago 1982: 99). This reading of a reading of the Brazilian cultural context is what allows Santiago to approach *Modernismo* as the overcoming of the model by the copy, a parodic appropriation of the discourse of the Same by the Other which subverts it. The paradigmatic example of *Macunaíma*, by Mário de Andrade, unveils the new manoeuvring space of the text-of-difference and of the struggle of the discordant voices of which it is made: 'It is in this barely peaceful in-between that the Brazilian intellectual finds today volcanic soil where he

In Conversation

may *un*repress all the values which were destroyed by the culture of the conquerors [...] that the novel writer sees in the mirror, not its reflected image, but that of the anthropologist [...] who does not have to leave his own country' (Santiago 1982: 39).

The issue of the copy does not exhaust itself, however, in the virulent act of desacralization, decentralization and deconstitution operated by parody, in the context of a country that sought, through modernization, a break with the old dominant oligarchies. Made into a commonplace, after its renewed upsurge in the *tropicalista* movement of the sixties, parody discourse loses its power of contestation and its *raison d'être* and is substituted in more recent years by pastiche. More than a mere artistic technique of appropriation of the discourse of the Other and a new fad from the dominant centres, pastiche is taken up by Santiago as an operational category which, by being clearly distinct from parody in its strong opposition to the past, allows it to hold a dialogue between past and present without being derogatory, in a space in which different and opposing elements live together, in a terrain where contradictory figures coexist.

It is possible to recover, more adequately, and without any kind of prejudice, the reason for the continuity of the discourse of tradition in modernism, which is not, of course, characterized by the use of pastiche. It is also on this horizon that the current manifestations of post-modernity are to be found amongst us, freed from the weight of the lessons of the 'wise and authoritarian fathers' (Santiago 1983) of modernity, and able to hold a dialogue which occurs with pillaging and pastiche to an infinite degree in the most varied styles in a pleasurable, sinful and transgressive relation with culture. This is not, of course, a neo-conservative reaction which intends to hide the problem of dependence by abandoning its contextualization. On the contrary, what is brought out — and here is the most consistent point of this critical breakthrough — is the idea of literary property. Previously owned at any cost, through the most varied cultural and ideological subterfuges, it declared us always to be in debt, always accountable to the librarians on duty. It remains to be seen how intellectual action opened the way for the change.

Another weight, other measures

In 'Calidoscópio de Questões' ['Kaleidoscope of Questions'], Santiago opens his text with an epigraph by Mário de Andrade:

Lines of criticism? Maybe. Sincere impressions, truths in which I believe, solutions I reached by the moving, loving reading of these Masters of the Past. (Santiago 1983b: 25)

As one reads further in the essay, the supplementary meaning that Andrade's words acquire in the new context unveils itself, as well as the scope for the project of the revision of *Modernismo* carried out by Santiago. The analogy is ironically expressive: just as in 1921, the São Paulo critic considered the cycle of Parnassian literary production to be over, with all that made it an obstacle to the development of Brazilian literature and that budding *Modernismo* was beginning to blow away, Santiago also considers another cycle of this culture — that of the '*modernista* tradition' — which, founded on the aesthetic conquests of 1922, was beginning, in turn, to act as a stumbling block to the new generation of writers who were affirming themselves by the seventies.

The handling of the issue, contrary to previous approaches, integrates the three presuppositions which neither the great historiographical syntheses of *Modernismo*, nor the critical reading of the most representative works of the movement, managed adequately to account for. The assumptions, as laid out in 'O Teorema de Walnice e a Sua Recíproca' ['Walnice's Theorem and its Reciprocal'], are: 'aesthetic (of the work itself), political (of the political action of the one who produces it) and civilising (of the public who reads the work)' (Santiago 1982: 84). The objectives pursued become very clear by the use as a tool of criticism of the 'lesser' parts of the *Modernista* production, which include memoirs and correspondence and had been undervalued until then. It is not only a question of outlining the strokes that define the subject inscribed in these texts and the strategy used to do so, but also of outlining a kind of history of the modernist minds able to account for the issue of the social and political participation of intellectuals in the thirties.

The contrasting analysis between the text of fiction and the text of memoirs shows clearly how the meaning of the modernist text and its discursive specificity is to be found in the gap between these two spheres. In this space, the revolutionary aesthetic break, linked to the progressive international parameters of the time, goes hand in hand with the restoration of the past and tradition that the memoir movement seeks to recover. Santiago's reading of the journey by Mário, Oswald, Tarsila and other *modernistas*, in the company of Blaise Cendrars, to the historical towns of Minas Gerais in 1924, is fundamental. The critic highlights the surprise of Tarsila when she saw the baroque paintings and sculptures and her desire to return to Paris, not after the latest Parisian fashion, but in order to learn to *restore* pictures (Santiago, 1989: 105ff.).

The individual identity of the subject of these memoirs derives from the recognition — very often jubilatory, as in Drummond de Andrade — of the values of the family and the patriarchal clan, inherent to a past which was thought dead or that *Modernismo* intended to bury forever. The socio-political identity of this subject, which reveals its ideological contradictions, derives from his commitment to the process of social modernization which results in the authoritarianism of the *Estado Novo*. In these terms, the analysis of Mário de Andrade's participation in the creation of a cultural project for the country is decisive, considering the establishment of rules of acceptance for public jobs by Andrade and the drawing up for himself of an ethics compatible with the *'trahison des clercs'*. The analysis fits the broader discussion of the role of the modernist intellectual *vis-à-vis* the market, the public and the government. As Santiago says, 'in his relation to the market he is an elitist; in his relation to the public, he is self-sufficient and authoritarian; in his relation to power he defends ways of governing that can be seen as autocratic' (Santiago 1983: 27).

Elitism, self-sufficiency and autocracy are outlined by Santiago from a particular joint approach to the processes of production and reception of the *Modernista* text. This clarifies both the lack of prestige attributed to the writer by the readers at the time, as well as the later recognition of the value and quality of his work. Since he was not a professional writer and did not depend on the editorial market for his living or for the legitimising of his work (something always done between peers), the modernist writer does not submit himself to the laws of the market or the reading habits of the common public, moving away from the latter by producing an elliptical text which discards any concession to the readers' tastes through a refusal to use 'popular' resources such as repetition and redundancy.

From this point of view, the modernist writer removes his work, as it were, from the more direct action of improving the cultural standards of the population, abdicating this responsibility out of the belief that the problem would be solved by the modernization of Brazilian society, which the political situation at the time was beginning to trigger: 'the adaptation of the modernist intellectual to the *"Estado Novo"* is related undoubtedly to his sympathy for authoritarianism and by the belief that the "backwardness" of the nation was — like it or not — being solved by the imposition of a dictatorship that was setting the right pace within the demands of progress' (Santiago 1983: 28).

From the guidelines provided by his analysis of a movement which has already passed into history, Santiago finds important indicators for the examination of a wider issue — that of the professionalization of the writer — which in turn helps underpin an understanding of Brazilian literature after 1964. In order to do this, the author uses the 'theorem of Walnice', which may be summarized in the observation that 'the writers most independent from the State in a free-enterprise regime are more dependent on the whims of the market' (Santiago 1982: 70). The effectiveness of the equation comes from the penetrating reading by Walnice Nogueira Galvão of the work of Jorge Amado and Érico Veríssimo and the observation that if, on the one hand, the contestatory behaviour of the work of each one is facilitated or made possible by the fact that their authors do not have ties of employment with the State (as opposed to what occurred with the modernists), on the other hand, the relation of dependence which both have on the consumer market is precisely what brings about the loss of artistic quality.

Santiago endorses Walnice's analysis of Amado's work, although he seeks to discuss the elitist concept of art which marks her statements and underpins her conclusions. This concept is questioned because she does not consider one of the manifold functions of the work of art, that of creating a reading public, which, as was seen earlier, *Modernismo* had no interest in doing. The formulation of such a theory by Santiago widens the discussion of the problem and seeks adequately to place and evaluate Brazilian literary production in the last two decades. The corresponding theory is made up of a wide range of issues that lead toward the broader question, 'if artistic deterioration and political rebellion were the perfect partners blessed by the free-enterprise system, will artistic competence and political complacency be the eternal couple blessed by the conservatism of the Brazilian intellectual elite?' (Santiago 1982: 80). The possibility of a categorically definite answer to the question remains open. But it is possible to bring in, as Santiago does, some facts that contribute toward an effective solution to the problem.

To escape economic dependence on the State and fall blindly into the hands of the market, in order to keep a politically independent attitude, is not a solution either for the artistic product or for its producer. To insist on the alibi of the dissociation between the artistic freedom of the work and the closeness of its producer to the State as a mere means of economic subsistence is not a solution either — this attitude, at most, helps to reinforce the schizophrenic division between the intellectual and the artist which can be seen in the case of the bureaucrat Drummond de Andrade working for the *Estado Novo* and as the committed poet of *A rosa do povo* [*People's Rose*] (1945).

In a country marked by illiteracy, poor schooling, limited cultural circulation, to mention only a few of the most relevant issues, it is not right to persist in demanding a reader laden with culture, from the elite, as idealized by the *modernistas*. It is also not right to adopt the universalising position which sees the artist as a temporary and provisional intellectual who only involves himself in the issues of his time when he is called upon to do so, returning, once he has accomplished his mission, to the 'alienation' of the production of his work.

Santiago's proposal to change this situation, given the accidents of history that Brazilian artists must constantly submit to, goes through a process of 'popularization' of art, which is not to be confused in any way with populist proposals that some attempts have erroneously tried to advance since the sixties. It presupposes, on the contrary, taking up again, by mere reflex, the positive aspects of the artistic and intellectual activity that writers such as Graciliano Ramos, Lima Barreto and Euclides da Cunha left to Brazilian literature: from Ramos, the courageous insistence not to separate the theory of art from the theory of life, of which the *Memórias do cárcere* [*Prison Memoirs*] are a haunting witness (this experiment is taken up by Santiago himself in the text *Em liberdade* [*In Liberty*]); from Lima Barreto, the use of the stylistic devices of the journalistic pamphleteers of the time and their creative transformation into a resource for the creation of a popular aesthetic for the novel; from da Cunha, his critical and lucid position in the face of a historical event crucial to Brazilian history. Or, in Santiago's words about the last two:

> If the great lesson of Lima Barreto is that of popular and, at the same time, critical writing, that of Euclides is one of a knowledge that, by detaching himself from the authoritarianism inherent to the group holding it and from himself, he turns his eyes on those who were beaten, finding in them a truth which escapes the excluding guidelines of modernization (Santiago 1989, 93).

Margins of joy

In view of what has been said, it is not difficult to understand the importance that the systematic thinking-through of post-'64 Brazilian literature has in Santiago's critical work and, further still, the gap that this thinking has filled, and not before time, in the overall picture of recent Brazilian criticism. If the rigorous attention given by Santiago to *Modernismo* results in an opening of paths to a fairer understanding of the Movement's legacy of contradictions and contributions to national culture, it is this attention that makes it possible to evaluate the process of flow and counterflow of current literary production in the face of an already established tradition. It is not a case of measuring through its parameters the potential of the young writers born of an aesthetic revolution in the recent past, or of a political military rebellion which is even more recent. That would result in the neutralization of this potential and in a mistaken and reactionary counterpoise to the freedom of research and aesthetic creation.

In his critical panorama of Brazilian literary prose in the last two decades, Santiago highlights the healthy 'formal anarchy' informing it, although he stresses two main lines which, at an early stage, are defined by the camouflaged or displaced approach to situations forbidden by censorship and the repression imposed by the military regime. It is the case of narrative with a highly metaphorical discourse and an oneiric-fantastic logic which, through disguise, radically criticizes the macro-structures of power and the authoritarian microstructures which prevail in day-to-day situations. It is the case of the reportage-novel which mimics journalistic language and therefore shifts the treatment of violence and the police arbitrariness of the time of the *AI-5* into the literary realm, denouncing what the newspapers and television could not express.[1]

With the return of the political exiles in the second half of the seventies, a new line — that of autobiographical text — achieves an unprecedented relevance within Brazilian culture. This is a determining factor in the literature of the time, although this line took up again, in a way, the memoir component which defined one of the most significant aspects of modernist prose. Even though the old modernists' late memoir production was still active at the time, sharing with the young former political exiles' autobiographical texts the fact that they were narratives of lived experience, Santiago underlines the basic differences between them. While the text of the old modernists is centred on the recovery of personal experience from its insertion into the history of the family and of the clan, the text of the young former exiles centres its interest on the individual and his participation in the small marginal group:

> [T]he text of the modernists, tracking a path we may call 'Proustian', tends to present a conservative view of Brazilian patriarchal society, told through the inertia of the main protagonist (whose prototype is

---

[1] The military government's Institutional Act number 5 — *AI-5* — introduced censorship and drastically reduced Brazilian citizens' individual freedom and civil rights.

In Conversation

the public employee); while the text of the young former exiles, admitting as almost non-existent the gap between the fact lived yesterday and its narration today, tells immediate and endured experiences, where what was at stake was the liberation of Brazil by armed struggle. (Santiago 1989: 33)

Through the comparison, Santiago finds basic resources to evaluate the current state of Brazilian literature, whether from a critico-historiographic point-of-view; or from a more theoretical cross-section, although both one and the other criss-cross in his argument. It is in this way that the strictly political issues raised by the first-person witness trigger the expression, through fiction and reports, of the experience of minority groups such as Indians, black people/negroes, homosexuals, workers, women and the old. The basic problem stated by the critic is not just that of the aesthetic validity of these works, but the apprehension of the extent to and the sense in which they contribute to the affirmation of *difference*, and therefore, to the questioning of the microstructures of domination which, after the period of dictatorship, continue to operate, in various forms and disguises, on the national scene.

It is then in the diversity of themes that Santiago finds one of the clearest characteristics of differentiation and originality of post-'64 Brazilian literature, when compared to the previous committed literature. This diversity expresses both a *mea culpa* for the failure of the revolution, carried out by the young autobiographers with the awareness that any effective social revolutionary project must include the sensual liberation of the individual, and a fulminating criticism of any form of authoritarianism, carried out by the emerging literary production of the minorities. The difference does not, however, restrict itself to uncovering the diversity of themes, drawn from the 'shocked and indignant discovery of the violence of power' (Santiago 1989: 16), but widens to an ideological understanding of the young artists' disbelief in and lack of commitment to totalizing and totalitarian development projects. This attitude was the opposite of that of the majority of writers of the generation of the thirties, right and left, who saw themselves involved together in projects of this nature. Because of this, the literary text 'no longer expresses itself by grandiose tones and by exercises of high rhetoric', preferring 'to insinuate itself, like cracks in concrete, with a low and amusing voice, in a minor and colloquial key' (Santiago 1989: 18).

In this critical conception, joy is not just another spot check, but a 'force majeure' (a term borrowed from Clément Rosset) that opens the doors of Brazilian literature to post-modernity, yet frees it of the weight of 'pure negativeness' and of the 'spirit of resentment'. 'People in power, contradictorily, were optimistic and sad. The opponents of the regime, affirmatively, were sacrificed and happy' (Santiago 1989: 23). The best way to understand with clarity the productive effectiveness and the scope of this position is to resort to the fiction-essay *Em liberdade* — a pretend-transcription by Santiago of the diary Graciliano Ramos supposedly wrote after leaving prison in 1937. In this daring project, the text enters a dialogue with the legacy of Ramos's work and with the literary production of the period in which Santiago writes.

The dramatization of the reading experience — achieved by the pastiche of autobiographical discourse — becomes fundamental. The narrator, now distanced from the life experience narrated and, at the same time, confused with it and mixing in it by transverse routes, dislodges the place of the subject of the *écriture*; in this way, he identifies with the reader in the look they together cast on the Other. During this interaction, or even at its beginning, a short-circuit interrupts and compromises the friendly relationship between them, when the reader notices that he is being deliberately cheated, since he cannot say for sure whose the diary is.

History against the grain (of the Walter Benjamin kind), without the illusion of the narrator's knowledge, slightly nostalgic and anachronistic, in a universe which is more and more informed by the mass media, *Em liberdade* is not, as the title itself says, a reverential funeral hymn. It is, on the contrary, the happy affirmation of an individual/individuals in the present, of firm resistance to all the past and future disorders, a healthy wind of renewal on the Brazilian literary scene.

The critical passion with which, at this point, the subject surrenders itself to the object, incorporates it at a distance, unfolds itself in it and does so to restore it with new life for the reader, is also, finally, what defines the critical direction of Santiago's thought —

> The double stiletto
> of the text and of the reading,
> of the author and of the reader.
>
> The double tattoo
> against its own body
> and crude reality. (Santiago 1978a: 125)

In Conversation

REFERENCES

Cândido, Antônio. 'Literatura e subdesenvolvimento', *Argumento* 1 (1973), 7-24.

Gomes, Paulo Emílio Salles. 'Cinema: trajetória no subdesenvovlvimento', *Argumento* 1 (1972), 55-67.

Miceli, Sérgio. *Intelectuais e classe dirigente no Brasil (1920-1945)* (São Paulo: Difel, 1979).

Rosset, Clément. *La force majeure* (Paris: Minuit, 1983).

Santiago, Silviano. 'A Palavra de Deus', *Barroco* 3 (1970a), 7-13.

Santiago, Silviano. *O banquete* (Rio de Janeiro: Saga, 1970b).

Santiago, Silviano. *Carlos Drummond de Andrade* (Petrópolis: Vozes, 1976).

Santiago, Silviano. *Crescendo durante a guerra numa província ultramarina* (Rio de Janeiro: Francisco Alves, 1978a).

Santiago, Silviano. *Uma literatura nos trópicos: ensaios sobre dependência cultural* (São Paulo: Perspectiva, 1978b).

Santiago, Silviano. *Em liberdade* (Rio de Janeiro: Paz e Terra, 1981).

Santiago, Silviano. *Vale quanto pesa: ensaios sobre questões político-culturais* (Rio de Janeiro: Paz e Terra, 1982).

Santiago, Silviano. 'Littérature: Morts les Parents Sages et Autoritaires', *Le monde diplomatique* (1983a).

Santiago, Silviano. 'Calidoscópio de Questões', *Sete ensaios sobre o modernismo* (Rio de Janeiro: MAC/FUNARTE, 1983b).

Santiago, Silviano. *Stella Manhattan* (Rio de Janeiro: Nova Fronteira, 1985).

Santiago, Silviano. *Nas malhas da letra: ensaios* (São Paulo: Companhia das Letras, 1989).

Schwarz, Roberto. *Ao vencedor as batatas* (São Paulo: Duas Cidades, 1977).

Schwarz, Roberto. *Que horas são?* (São Paulo: Companhia das Letras, 1987).

Süssekind, Flora. 'Reflexão tática', *34 Letras* 1 (1988), 84-9.

SILVIANO SANTIAGO:
a Bibliographical Note

A full bibliography of works by and on Silviano Santiago, in Portuguese and other languages, appears in Wander Melo Miranda and Eneida Maria de Souza (eds.), *Navegar é preciso, viver: escritos para Silviano Santiago* (Belo Horizonte: Editora UFMG, Salvador: EDUFBA; Niterói: EDUFF, 1997), 337-61.

His principal works of fiction are:

Duas Faces [with Ivan Ângelo] (Belo Horizonte: Ed. Itatiaia, 1961)
O banquete (Rio de Janeiro: Saga, 1970)
O olhar (Belo Horizonte: Tendência, 1974)
Em liberdade (Rio de Janeiro: Nova Fronteira, 1985)
Uma história de família (Rio de Janeiro: Rocco, 1992)
Viagem ao México (Rio de Janeiro: Rocco, 1995)
Keith Jarrett no Blue Note (Rio de Janeiro: Rocco, 1995)
Decócoras (Rio de Janeiro: Rocco, 1999)

MACDONALD DALY is Senior Lecturer and Director of Research in the Postgraduate School of Critical Theory and Cultural Studies, University of Nottingham.

ELSE R P VIEIRA is Associate Professor at the Federal University of Minas Gerais, and is a Visiting Fellow of the Centre for Brazilian Studies, University of Oxford.

WANDER MELO MIRANDA is Professor of Critical Theory at the Federal University of Minas Gerais. He is also the Director of the UFMG University Press.

K DAVID JACKSON is Professor in Portuguese and Brazilian Literature at Yale University. His many publications include *A Hidden Presence: 500 Years of Portuguese Culture in India and Sri Lanka* (1995).

BERNARD MCGUIRK is Professor of Romance Literatures and Literary Theory in the University of Nottingham. He is Head of the Postgraduate School of Critical Theory and Cultural Studies.

RICHARD KING is Professor of American Intellectual History in the School of American and Canadian Studies at the University of Nottingham.

www.ingramcontent.com/pod-product-compliance
Lightning Source LLC
Chambersburg PA
CBHW021942040426
42448CB00008B/1188